50 Thailand Lunch Recipes for Home

By: Kelly Johnson

Table of Contents

- Pad Thai
- Tom Yum Soup
- Green Curry
- Mango Sticky Rice
- Massaman Curry
- Thai Basil Chicken (Pad Krapow Gai)
- Som Tum (Green Papaya Salad)
- Red Curry
- Chicken Satay with Peanut Sauce
- Tom Kha Gai (Coconut Chicken Soup)
- Pad See Ew (Stir-Fried Noodles)
- Thai Fried Rice
- Larb (Minced Meat Salad)
- Panang Curry
- Thai Spring Rolls
- Pineapple Fried Rice
- Thai Fish Cakes (Tod Mun Pla)
- Khao Soi (Northern Thai Curry Noodles)
- Thai Beef Salad
- Pad Kee Mao (Drunken Noodles)
- Thai Crab Curry
- Thai Chicken Green Curry Fried Rice
- Thai Grilled Chicken (Gai Yang)
- Thai Pork Satay
- Stir-Fried Morning Glory (Pad Pak Boong Fai Daeng)
- Thai Shrimp Cakes
- Thai Pumpkin Curry
- Thai Basil Eggplant
- Thai Glass Noodle Salad (Yum Woon Sen)
- Thai Cucumber Salad
- Thai Coconut Soup (Tom Kha)
- Thai Fried Chicken
- Thai Sweet Chili Sauce
- Thai Garlic Shrimp
- Thai Basil Fried Rice

- Thai BBQ Pork (Moo Ping)
- Thai Stir-Fried Vegetables
- Thai Crab Fried Rice
- Thai Cashew Chicken
- Thai Green Papaya Salad (Som Tum)
- Thai Peanut Sauce
- Thai Steamed Fish with Lime and Garlic
- Thai Beef Noodle Soup (Kuay Teow Neua)
- Thai Omelette (Kai Jeow)
- Thai Coconut Pudding (Tub Tim Grob)
- Thai Spicy Pork Salad (Nam Tok Moo)
- Thai Stir-Fried Tofu with Basil
- Thai Chicken Curry Noodles (Khao Soi Gai)
- Thai Green Bean Salad
- Thai Pineapple Fried Rice

Pad Thai

Ingredients:

- 8 oz (225g) rice noodles
- 2 tbsp vegetable oil
- 1 shallot, finely chopped
- 2 cloves garlic, minced
- 1/2 cup tofu, cut into small cubes
- 1/2 cup shrimp, peeled and deveined (optional)
- 2 eggs, lightly beaten
- 2 cups bean sprouts
- 3 green onions, chopped
- 1/4 cup crushed peanuts
- Lime wedges (for serving)
- Fresh cilantro (for garnish)

For the sauce:

- 3 tbsp tamarind paste
- 3 tbsp fish sauce
- 2 tbsp soy sauce
- 2 tbsp brown sugar
- 1/4 tsp chili flakes (optional)

Instructions:

1. **Prepare the noodles:** Cook the rice noodles according to package instructions until they are just tender. Drain and set aside.
2. **Make the sauce:** In a small bowl, mix together tamarind paste, fish sauce, soy sauce, brown sugar, and chili flakes until well combined. Adjust the sweetness or saltiness to taste.
3. **Stir-fry:** Heat vegetable oil in a large pan or wok over medium-high heat. Add shallot and garlic, and sauté until fragrant.
4. **Cook tofu and shrimp:** Push the shallot and garlic to the side of the pan. Add tofu and shrimp (if using) to the center of the pan and cook until shrimp turns pink and tofu is lightly browned.
5. **Add eggs:** Push everything to the side of the pan again, and pour the beaten eggs into the center. Scramble the eggs until they are fully cooked.
6. **Combine everything:** Add the cooked noodles to the pan along with the prepared sauce. Toss everything together until the noodles are well coated with the sauce.
7. **Add bean sprouts and green onions:** Stir in bean sprouts and green onions, and cook for another minute until the bean sprouts are slightly wilted.
8. **Serve:** Remove from heat and transfer Pad Thai to serving plates. Sprinkle crushed peanuts on top and garnish with lime wedges and fresh cilantro.

9. **Enjoy:** Serve immediately and enjoy your homemade Pad Thai!

Feel free to adjust the ingredients and seasonings according to your taste preferences. Pad Thai is versatile, and you can add more vegetables or protein as desired.

Tom Yum Soup

Ingredients:

- 4 cups chicken or vegetable broth
- 2 lemongrass stalks, cut into 2-inch pieces and lightly smashed
- 3-4 kaffir lime leaves, torn into pieces
- 3-4 slices galangal (Thai ginger)
- 3-4 Thai bird's eye chilies, smashed (adjust amount to your spice preference)
- 200g shrimp, peeled and deveined (or chicken breast/tofu)
- 200g mushrooms (straw mushrooms or button mushrooms), sliced
- 2 tomatoes, cut into wedges
- 1 onion, thinly sliced
- 2 tbsp fish sauce
- 1-2 tbsp lime juice
- 1 tbsp chili paste in oil (optional, for extra heat)
- Fresh cilantro leaves, for garnish
- Thai basil leaves, for garnish (optional)

Instructions:

1. **Prepare the broth:** In a pot, bring the chicken or vegetable broth to a boil over medium-high heat.
2. **Infuse flavors:** Add lemongrass, kaffir lime leaves, galangal, and Thai bird's eye chilies to the broth. Simmer for about 5-7 minutes to allow the flavors to infuse into the broth.
3. **Add protein and vegetables:** Add shrimp (or chicken/tofu), mushrooms, tomatoes, and onion to the pot. Cook until shrimp turns pink and opaque (or chicken/tofu is cooked through), about 3-5 minutes.
4. **Season:** Stir in fish sauce, lime juice, and chili paste in oil (if using). Taste and adjust the seasoning as needed. The soup should have a balance of spicy, sour, salty, and slightly sweet flavors.
5. **Serve:** Remove from heat and discard lemongrass stalks and galangal slices. Ladle the soup into serving bowls. Garnish with fresh cilantro leaves and Thai basil leaves (if using).
6. **Enjoy:** Serve hot as a starter or main dish with steamed rice.

Note: Tom Yum Soup is highly customizable. You can adjust the level of spiciness by adding more or fewer Thai bird's eye chilies, and you can add additional vegetables like baby corn, bell peppers, or bok choy to suit your preferences. This soup is best enjoyed fresh and hot, straight from the pot!

Green Curry

Ingredients:

- 1 can (14 oz) coconut milk
- 2-3 tbsp green curry paste (store-bought or homemade)
- 1 lb chicken breast or thighs, thinly sliced (or protein of your choice)
- 1 cup bamboo shoots, sliced (optional)
- 1 red bell pepper, sliced
- 1 eggplant, cut into bite-sized pieces
- 1 cup Thai basil leaves
- 2 tbsp fish sauce
- 1 tbsp palm sugar or brown sugar
- 1-2 kaffir lime leaves, torn
- 1/2 cup chicken or vegetable broth (optional, for thinner consistency)
- Fresh Thai basil leaves, for garnish (optional)

For the green curry paste (if making from scratch):

- 1-2 green Thai chilies, chopped (adjust to your spice preference)
- 1 shallot, chopped
- 3 cloves garlic, chopped
- 1 stalk lemongrass, thinly sliced
- 1-inch piece galangal, chopped (or substitute with ginger)
- 1 tbsp chopped cilantro stems
- 1/2 tsp ground cumin
- 1/2 tsp ground coriander
- 1/4 tsp ground white pepper
- 1/4 tsp shrimp paste (optional)
- Zest of 1 kaffir lime (or substitute with lime zest)

Instructions:

1. **Prepare the curry paste (if making from scratch):** In a mortar and pestle or a food processor, grind together all the ingredients for the green curry paste until smooth. Set aside.
2. **Cooking the curry:**
    - Heat a large pan or wok over medium heat. Add about half of the coconut milk (the thicker top part if it's separated) and stir until it starts to bubble.
    - Add the green curry paste to the pan and stir-fry for 1-2 minutes until fragrant.
    - Add the sliced chicken (or other protein) to the pan and cook until it is no longer pink on the outside.
    - Pour in the remaining coconut milk and chicken or vegetable broth (if using), stirring to combine.

- - Add bamboo shoots (if using), red bell pepper, eggplant, and torn kaffir lime leaves to the pan. Simmer gently until the vegetables are tender and the chicken is fully cooked, about 10-15 minutes.
  - Season the curry with fish sauce and palm sugar (adjust to taste for saltiness and sweetness).
  - Stir in Thai basil leaves and cook for another minute until wilted.
3. **Serve:** Remove from heat and discard any whole kaffir lime leaves. Serve hot over steamed rice, garnished with fresh Thai basil leaves if desired.

Enjoy your homemade Green Curry, packed with aromatic flavors and a perfect balance of heat, sweetness, and creaminess from the coconut milk!

Mango Sticky Rice

Ingredients:

- 1 cup glutinous rice (also called sticky rice)
- 1 can (14 oz) coconut milk
- 1/2 cup granulated sugar
- 1/2 tsp salt
- 2 ripe mangoes, peeled and sliced
- Toasted sesame seeds or mung beans (optional, for garnish)

Instructions:

1. **Soak the sticky rice:**
   - Rinse the glutinous rice thoroughly under cold water until the water runs clear. Soak the rice in enough water to cover it for at least 4 hours or overnight.
2. **Steam the sticky rice:**
   - Drain the soaked rice and place it in a steamer lined with cheesecloth or a muslin cloth. Steam the rice over medium-high heat for about 25-30 minutes, or until the rice is tender and cooked through.
3. **Prepare the coconut sauce:**
   - While the rice is steaming, prepare the coconut sauce. In a saucepan, combine the coconut milk, sugar, and salt. Heat over medium heat, stirring occasionally, until the sugar has dissolved and the mixture is smooth. Do not boil.
4. **Mix the sticky rice with coconut sauce:**
   - Transfer the cooked sticky rice to a bowl. Gradually pour half of the warm coconut sauce over the rice, stirring gently to coat the rice evenly. Let the rice absorb the sauce for about 10 minutes.
5. **Assemble the dessert:**
   - Arrange slices of ripe mango on a serving plate or bowl.
   - Spoon portions of the coconut sticky rice next to the mango slices.
   - Drizzle the remaining coconut sauce over the mango and rice.
6. **Garnish and serve:**
   - Optional: Sprinkle toasted sesame seeds or mung beans on top for added texture and flavor.
   - Serve the Mango Sticky Rice warm or at room temperature.

Enjoy this delightful Thai dessert that captures the essence of tropical flavors with its creamy coconut rice and sweet mangoes!

Massaman Curry

Ingredients:

- 1 lb beef (such as chuck roast), cut into bite-sized pieces
- 2 cups coconut milk
- 2-3 tbsp Massaman curry paste (store-bought or homemade)
- 1 onion, sliced
- 2 potatoes, peeled and cut into chunks
- 1/2 cup roasted peanuts
- 2 tbsp fish sauce
- 1 tbsp palm sugar or brown sugar
- 1 cinnamon stick
- 3-4 cardamom pods, lightly crushed
- 3-4 whole cloves
- 1-2 star anise
- 1-2 bay leaves
- 1 cup chicken or beef broth (optional, for thinner consistency)
- Fresh cilantro leaves, for garnish
- Lime wedges, for serving
- Cooked jasmine rice, for serving

Instructions:

1. **Brown the beef:**
    - Heat a large pot or Dutch oven over medium-high heat. Add a bit of oil and brown the beef pieces on all sides. Remove the beef from the pot and set aside.
2. **Prepare the curry base:**
    - In the same pot, add a bit more oil if needed. Add the Massaman curry paste and stir-fry for about 1-2 minutes until fragrant.
3. **Simmer the curry:**
    - Pour in about half of the coconut milk, stirring to combine with the curry paste. Bring to a simmer.
    - Add the browned beef back into the pot, along with the remaining coconut milk, onion slices, potatoes, roasted peanuts, fish sauce, palm sugar, and the whole spices (cinnamon stick, cardamom pods, cloves, star anise, and bay leaves).
    - If using, add chicken or beef broth to achieve your desired consistency.
4. **Cook the curry:**
    - Cover the pot and simmer over low to medium heat for about 1.5 to 2 hours, or until the beef is tender and the potatoes are cooked through. Stir occasionally to prevent sticking and to ensure even cooking.
5. **Adjust seasoning:**
    - Taste the curry and adjust the seasoning with more fish sauce for saltiness or more sugar for sweetness, if needed.
6. **Serve:**

- Remove the whole spices (cinnamon stick, cardamom pods, cloves, star anise, and bay leaves) before serving.
- Garnish with fresh cilantro leaves.
- Serve hot with jasmine rice and lime wedges on the side.

Enjoy the rich and aromatic flavors of Massaman Curry, a comforting dish that blends Thai spices with creamy coconut milk for a delightful meal experience.

Thai Basil Chicken (Pad Krapow Gai)

Ingredients:

- 1 lb boneless, skinless chicken thighs or breasts, thinly sliced
- 2 tbsp vegetable oil
- 4-5 cloves garlic, minced
- 2-3 Thai bird's eye chilies, finely chopped (adjust to your spice preference)
- 1 red bell pepper, thinly sliced
- 1 onion, thinly sliced
- 1 cup fresh Thai basil leaves
- 2 tbsp oyster sauce
- 1 tbsp soy sauce
- 1 tbsp fish sauce
- 1 tsp sugar
- Freshly ground black pepper
- Cooked jasmine rice, for serving
- Fried egg (optional), for serving

Instructions:

1. **Prepare the sauce:** In a small bowl, mix together oyster sauce, soy sauce, fish sauce, sugar, and a dash of freshly ground black pepper. Set aside.
2. **Stir-fry the chicken:**
   - Heat vegetable oil in a wok or large skillet over medium-high heat.
   - Add minced garlic and chopped Thai bird's eye chilies. Stir-fry for about 30 seconds until fragrant.
   - Add thinly sliced chicken to the wok in a single layer. Let it cook undisturbed for 1-2 minutes to sear one side, then stir-fry for another 2-3 minutes until the chicken is cooked through and slightly browned.
3. **Add vegetables:**
   - Add thinly sliced red bell pepper and onion to the wok. Stir-fry for another 2-3 minutes until the vegetables are tender-crisp.
4. **Combine everything:**
   - Pour the prepared sauce over the chicken and vegetables in the wok. Stir well to coat everything evenly with the sauce.
5. **Add Thai basil:**
   - Remove the wok from heat and add fresh Thai basil leaves. Toss everything together until the basil leaves wilt slightly from the residual heat.
6. **Serve:**
   - Serve hot over steamed jasmine rice.
   - Optionally, serve with a fried egg on top for extra richness and flavor.

Enjoy this flavorful Thai Basil Chicken (Pad Krapow Gai) as a quick and satisfying meal that captures the essence of Thai cuisine with its bold flavors and aromatic basil.

Som Tum (Green Papaya Salad)

Ingredients:

- 1 small green papaya (about 1 lb), peeled and shredded
- 2-3 cloves garlic
- 2-3 Thai bird's eye chilies (adjust to taste)
- 2 tbsp roasted peanuts
- 1 cup cherry tomatoes, halved
- 1-2 cups long beans or green beans, cut into 1-inch pieces
- 2 tbsp fish sauce
- 2 tbsp lime juice
- 1 tbsp palm sugar or granulated sugar
- Optional: 1-2 tbsp dried shrimp (lightly toasted)

Instructions:

1. **Prepare the papaya:** Peel the green papaya and cut it in half. Remove the seeds with a spoon and shred the papaya using a julienne peeler or a grater. Place the shredded papaya in a large mixing bowl.
2. **Make the dressing:** In a mortar and pestle, pound the garlic and Thai bird's eye chilies together until they form a rough paste. If you don't have a mortar and pestle, you can finely mince them with a knife.
3. **Combine ingredients:** Add the roasted peanuts, cherry tomatoes, and long beans (or green beans) to the bowl with the shredded papaya.
4. **Prepare the dressing:** In a small bowl, mix together fish sauce, lime juice, and palm sugar (or granulated sugar) until the sugar dissolves.
5. **Assemble the salad:** Pour the dressing over the papaya mixture in the bowl. If using dried shrimp, add them now. Toss everything together gently but thoroughly to ensure the dressing coats all the ingredients.
6. **Serve:** Transfer the Som Tum to a serving plate or bowl. Garnish with extra peanuts and fresh herbs if desired. Serve immediately as a refreshing appetizer or side dish.

Som Tum is best enjoyed fresh and can be adjusted to suit your taste preferences for spiciness and sweetness. It's a wonderful balance of flavors and textures, perfect for hot days or alongside your favorite Thai dishes!

Som Tum (Green Papaya Salad)

Ingredients:

- 1 green papaya, peeled and shredded
- 2-3 cloves garlic
- 2-3 Thai chilies (adjust according to spice preference)
- 2 tablespoons roasted peanuts
- 1-2 tablespoons dried shrimp (optional)
- 1-2 tablespoons palm sugar (or brown sugar)
- 2 tablespoons fish sauce
- 3-4 tablespoons lime juice
- 1-2 tomatoes, cut into wedges
- Long beans (optional), cut into 2-inch pieces
- Carrot (optional), julienned
- Cabbage leaves (optional), for serving

Instructions:

1. **Prepare Papaya**: Peel the green papaya and shred it using a grater or a julienne peeler. Place the shredded papaya in a large mixing bowl.
2. **Make Dressing**: In a mortar and pestle, pound garlic and Thai chilies together until they form a coarse paste. Add roasted peanuts and pound lightly until slightly crushed.
3. **Combine Ingredients**: Add dried shrimp (if using), palm sugar, fish sauce, and lime juice to the mortar. Mix everything together well.
4. **Mix Salad**: Pour the dressing over the shredded papaya in the mixing bowl. Toss everything together gently using a spoon or your hands, ensuring the papaya is well coated with the dressing.
5. **Add Vegetables**: Add tomato wedges, long beans (if using), julienned carrot (if using), and toss gently again.
6. **Serve**: Transfer the salad to a serving plate lined with cabbage leaves (optional) to serve.

Notes:

- **Adjust Heat**: The spiciness of Som Tum can be adjusted by varying the amount of Thai chilies used.
- **Texture**: The salad should be crunchy and tangy with a hint of sweetness from palm sugar.
- **Variations**: Some variations include adding slices of cucumber, green beans, or even adding a bit of tamarind paste for extra tanginess.

Som Tum is typically served as a side dish with sticky rice and grilled meats, such as chicken or pork. It's a vibrant and flavorful salad that showcases the balance of Thai cuisine's key flavors: spicy, sour, salty, and sweet.

Red Curry

Ingredients:

- 1 tablespoon vegetable oil
- 2-3 tablespoons red curry paste (adjust to your spice preference)
- 1 can (14 oz) coconut milk
- 1 cup chicken broth or vegetable broth
- 1 lb chicken breast or thighs, thinly sliced (or substitute with shrimp, beef, tofu, or vegetables)
- 1 red bell pepper, thinly sliced
- 1 onion, thinly sliced
- 1 cup bamboo shoots (optional)
- 1 cup baby corn (optional)
- 1 tablespoon fish sauce (or soy sauce for vegetarian)
- 1 tablespoon brown sugar (optional, to balance flavors)
- Thai basil leaves or cilantro for garnish
- Cooked rice for serving

Instructions:

1. Heat vegetable oil in a large skillet or wok over medium-high heat.
2. Add red curry paste to the skillet and stir-fry for about 1-2 minutes until fragrant.
3. Pour in the coconut milk and chicken broth, stirring until well combined and bringing it to a simmer.
4. Add the thinly sliced chicken (or your choice of protein) to the skillet and cook for 5-7 minutes until the chicken is cooked through.
5. Add the sliced red bell pepper, onion, bamboo shoots, and baby corn (if using). Cook for another 3-5 minutes until the vegetables are tender-crisp.
6. Season the curry with fish sauce and brown sugar, adjusting to taste. Stir well to combine.
7. Remove the skillet from heat. Taste and adjust seasoning if needed.
8. Serve the red curry hot over cooked rice, garnished with Thai basil leaves or cilantro.

Enjoy your homemade Thai Red Curry! Adjust the spiciness by varying the amount of red curry paste used.

Chicken Satay with Peanut Sauce

Ingredients:

For the Chicken Satay:

- 1 lb chicken breast or thighs, cut into thin strips
- 1 tablespoon soy sauce
- 1 tablespoon fish sauce
- 1 tablespoon curry powder
- 1 tablespoon brown sugar
- 1 tablespoon vegetable oil
- Bamboo skewers, soaked in water for 30 minutes

For the Peanut Sauce:

- 1/2 cup creamy peanut butter
- 1/4 cup coconut milk
- 2 tablespoons soy sauce
- 1 tablespoon brown sugar
- 1 tablespoon lime juice
- 1 teaspoon grated ginger
- 1 clove garlic, minced
- 1/2 teaspoon red pepper flakes (optional, for spiciness)
- Water (as needed to adjust consistency)

For Serving:

- Chopped peanuts, cilantro, and lime wedges for garnish
- Cooked rice or flatbread (optional)

Instructions:

1. **Marinate the Chicken:**
   - In a bowl, mix together soy sauce, fish sauce, curry powder, brown sugar, and vegetable oil.
   - Add the chicken strips to the marinade, ensuring they are well coated. Cover and refrigerate for at least 30 minutes (or up to 2 hours) to marinate.
2. **Prepare the Peanut Sauce:**
   - In a saucepan over medium heat, combine peanut butter, coconut milk, soy sauce, brown sugar, lime juice, grated ginger, minced garlic, and red pepper flakes (if using).
   - Stir continuously until the sauce is smooth and heated through. If the sauce is too thick, add water gradually to reach desired consistency. Remove from heat and set aside.
3. **Skewer and Grill the Chicken:**

- Preheat your grill or grill pan over medium-high heat.
- Thread marinated chicken strips onto soaked bamboo skewers, shaking off excess marinade.
- Grill the chicken skewers for about 3-4 minutes per side, or until cooked through and nicely charred. Cooking time may vary depending on the thickness of your chicken strips.

4. **Serve:**
    - Arrange the grilled chicken satay skewers on a serving platter.
    - Serve with the prepared peanut sauce on the side for dipping.
    - Garnish with chopped peanuts, cilantro, and lime wedges.
    - Optionally, serve with cooked rice or flatbread.

Enjoy your delicious Chicken Satay with Peanut Sauce! It's perfect as an appetizer or main dish for any occasion. Adjust the spice level of the peanut sauce to your preference by adding more or less red pepper flakes.

Tom Kha Gai (Coconut Chicken Soup)

Ingredients:

- 1 lb chicken breasts or thighs, thinly sliced
- 4 cups chicken broth
- 1 can (14 oz) coconut milk
- 1 lemongrass stalk, cut into 2-inch pieces and bruised
- 3-4 slices galangal or ginger (about 1 inch each)
- 4-5 kaffir lime leaves, torn or finely sliced
- 2-3 red Thai bird's eye chilies, sliced (adjust to spice preference)
- 1 medium onion, thinly sliced
- 1 cup sliced mushrooms (such as straw mushrooms or button mushrooms)
- 1 medium tomato, cut into wedges
- 2 tablespoons fish sauce (adjust to taste)
- 1 tablespoon sugar
- 2 tablespoons lime juice
- Fresh cilantro leaves for garnish
- Optional: Thai basil leaves for garnish

Instructions:

1. **Prepare the Broth:**
    - In a large pot, bring the chicken broth to a boil over medium-high heat.
    - Add lemongrass, galangal or ginger slices, and torn kaffir lime leaves. Simmer for about 5-10 minutes to infuse the flavors into the broth.
2. **Add Chicken and Vegetables:**
    - Add the thinly sliced chicken to the pot and cook until the chicken is cooked through, about 5-7 minutes.
3. **Add Coconut Milk and Vegetables:**
    - Stir in the coconut milk, sliced onion, mushrooms, and tomato wedges. Simmer for another 5 minutes, or until the vegetables are tender.
4. **Season the Soup:**
    - Stir in fish sauce, sugar, and sliced Thai bird's eye chilies. Adjust the seasoning with more fish sauce or sugar if needed, to achieve a balance of salty, sweet, and sour flavors.
5. **Finish and Serve:**
    - Remove the pot from heat and stir in lime juice. Taste and adjust the flavors according to your preference.
    - Ladle the Tom Kha Gai into serving bowls.
    - Garnish with fresh cilantro leaves and Thai basil leaves, if using.

Enjoy your homemade Tom Kha Gai! Serve it hot as a comforting and flavorful soup, perfect with steamed rice or on its own as a light meal. Adjust the spiciness by varying the amount of Thai bird's eye chilies used.

Pad See Ew (Stir-Fried Noodles)

Ingredients:

- 8 oz wide rice noodles
- 2 tablespoons vegetable oil
- 1/2 lb chicken breast or thighs, thinly sliced (or substitute with beef, pork, shrimp, or tofu)
- 2 cloves garlic, minced
- 1 cup Chinese broccoli (gai lan) or broccoli florets
- 1 egg, lightly beaten
- 2 tablespoons soy sauce
- 1 tablespoon oyster sauce
- 1 tablespoon fish sauce
- 1 tablespoon brown sugar
- White pepper, to taste
- Optional: sliced chili peppers in vinegar for serving

Instructions:

1. **Prepare the Rice Noodles:**
   - Cook the wide rice noodles according to package instructions until they are just tender. Drain and rinse with cold water to prevent sticking. Set aside.
2. **Prepare the Sauce:**
   - In a small bowl, mix together soy sauce, oyster sauce, fish sauce, and brown sugar until well combined. Set aside.
3. **Stir-Fry the Ingredients:**
   - Heat vegetable oil in a large wok or skillet over medium-high heat.
   - Add minced garlic and stir-fry for about 30 seconds until fragrant.
   - Add the thinly sliced chicken (or other protein) to the wok and cook until it is almost cooked through, about 3-4 minutes.
4. **Add Vegetables and Noodles:**
   - Push the chicken to one side of the wok. Crack the egg into the empty space and scramble it until cooked.
   - Add Chinese broccoli (or broccoli florets) to the wok and stir-fry for 1-2 minutes until they start to soften.
   - Add the cooked rice noodles to the wok along with the prepared sauce. Use tongs or chopsticks to gently toss everything together, ensuring the noodles are evenly coated with the sauce. Stir-fry for another 2-3 minutes until everything is heated through and well combined.
5. **Adjust Seasoning and Serve:**
   - Taste the Pad See Ew and adjust the seasoning if needed. Add white pepper to taste for a bit of heat.
   - Serve hot, optionally garnished with sliced chili peppers in vinegar on the side.

Enjoy your homemade Pad See Ew! It's a comforting and flavorful dish that's perfect for any meal. Adjust the ingredients and protein choice according to your preferences.

Thai Fried Rice

Ingredients:

- 3 cups cooked jasmine rice (preferably leftover and cooled)
- 2 tablespoons vegetable oil
- 2 cloves garlic, minced
- 1/2 cup protein of your choice (chicken, shrimp, pork, tofu, or a combination), diced or thinly sliced
- 1/2 cup mixed vegetables (such as carrots, peas, and corn)
- 2 eggs, lightly beaten
- 2 tablespoons soy sauce
- 1 tablespoon fish sauce
- 1 tablespoon oyster sauce
- 1 tablespoon sugar
- 1/4 teaspoon white pepper
- Green onions, chopped, for garnish
- Fresh cilantro, chopped, for garnish
- Lime wedges, for serving

Instructions:

1. **Prepare the Ingredients:**
    - If you haven't already, cook the jasmine rice and allow it to cool completely. Leftover rice works best for fried rice as it's less sticky.
2. **Stir-Fry the Ingredients:**
    - Heat vegetable oil in a wok or large skillet over medium-high heat.
    - Add minced garlic and stir-fry for about 30 seconds until fragrant.
    - Add your protein choice (chicken, shrimp, pork, tofu, etc.) and stir-fry until cooked through.
3. **Add Vegetables and Eggs:**
    - Push the cooked protein to the side of the wok. Pour the lightly beaten eggs into the empty space and scramble until just cooked.
4. **Combine Everything:**
    - Add the mixed vegetables to the wok and stir-fry for another minute until they are heated through.
    - Add the cooked jasmine rice to the wok, breaking up any clumps with a spatula or spoon.
5. **Season the Fried Rice:**
    - Drizzle soy sauce, fish sauce, and oyster sauce evenly over the rice. Sprinkle sugar and white pepper over the rice as well.
    - Use a spatula or spoon to gently toss and stir-fry the rice and other ingredients together until everything is well combined and heated through. Make sure the sauces are evenly distributed.
6. **Serve:**

- Transfer the Thai Fried Rice to serving plates or bowls.
- Garnish with chopped green onions and fresh cilantro.
- Serve hot with lime wedges on the side for squeezing over the rice.

Enjoy your homemade Thai Fried Rice! It's a versatile dish that can be customized with your favorite protein and vegetables. Adjust the seasoning according to your taste preferences.

Larb (zinced Meat Salad)

Ingredients:

- 1 lb ground pork (or chicken, beef, or duck)
- 2 tablespoons vegetable oil
- 2 shallots, thinly sliced
- 3-4 cloves garlic, minced
- 2-3 Thai bird's eye chilies, thinly sliced (adjust to your spice preference)
- 2 tablespoons fish sauce
- 2 tablespoons lime juice
- 1 tablespoon sugar
- 1/2 cup fresh mint leaves, chopped
- 1/2 cup fresh cilantro leaves, chopped
- 1/4 cup green onions, thinly sliced
- 2 tablespoons toasted rice powder (see note below)
- Fresh lettuce leaves, cucumber slices, and sticky rice for serving

Instructions:

1. **Cook the Ground Pork:**
    - Heat vegetable oil in a large skillet or wok over medium-high heat.
    - Add minced garlic and sliced shallots, and stir-fry for 1-2 minutes until fragrant.
    - Add ground pork to the skillet and cook, breaking it up with a spoon, until it is fully cooked and browned.
2. **Season the Larb:**
    - Reduce the heat to medium. Add Thai bird's eye chilies (adjust amount to your spice preference), fish sauce, lime juice, and sugar to the skillet. Stir well to combine and let it simmer for another minute.
3. **Add Fresh Herbs:**
    - Remove the skillet from heat. Stir in chopped mint leaves, cilantro leaves, and sliced green onions. These fresh herbs add brightness and flavor to the dish.
4. **Prepare Toasted Rice Powder:**
    - To make toasted rice powder, dry roast raw sticky rice in a pan over medium heat until golden brown, then grind it into a coarse powder using a spice grinder or mortar and pestle.
5. **Serve:**
    - Transfer the Larb to a serving dish.
    - Sprinkle toasted rice powder over the top of the Larb just before serving.
    - Serve Larb with fresh lettuce leaves, cucumber slices, and sticky rice on the side.

Notes:

- Larb is often served at room temperature or slightly warm.

- You can adjust the seasoning of Larb to your taste by adding more fish sauce, lime juice, or sugar as needed.
- If you prefer a vegetarian version, you can substitute the ground meat with crumbled tofu or mushrooms.

Enjoy your flavorful and aromatic Pork Larb! It's a refreshing and delicious dish that's perfect as an appetizer or main course.

Panang Curry

Ingredients:

For the Panang Curry Paste:

- 4-5 dried red chilies, soaked in warm water for 15-20 minutes
- 3 cloves garlic, peeled
- 2 shallots, peeled and chopped
- 1 stalk lemongrass, white part only, thinly sliced
- 1 inch piece galangal (or ginger), peeled and chopped
- 1 tablespoon coriander seeds, toasted and ground
- 1 teaspoon cumin seeds, toasted and ground
- 1/2 teaspoon shrimp paste (optional, for authentic flavor)
- 2-3 kaffir lime leaves, finely chopped (optional)
- 1 tablespoon vegetable oil

For the Curry:

- 1 lb chicken breast or thighs, thinly sliced (or substitute with beef, shrimp, or tofu)
- 1 can (14 oz) coconut milk
- 1/2 cup chicken broth or vegetable broth
- 2 tablespoons Panang curry paste (adjust to taste)
- 1 tablespoon fish sauce
- 1 tablespoon brown sugar (or palm sugar)
- 1 red bell pepper, thinly sliced
- 1/2 cup green beans, cut into 1-inch pieces
- Fresh Thai basil leaves for garnish (optional)

Instructions:

1. Make the Panang Curry Paste:

- Drain the soaked dried red chilies and roughly chop them.
- In a food processor or blender, combine the chopped red chilies, garlic, shallots, lemongrass, galangal, ground coriander, ground cumin, shrimp paste (if using), and kaffir lime leaves (if using).
- Process into a smooth paste, adding vegetable oil as needed to facilitate blending.

2. Prepare the Curry:

- Heat a large skillet or wok over medium-high heat. Add a tablespoon of vegetable oil.
- Add the Panang curry paste to the skillet and stir-fry for 1-2 minutes until fragrant.

3. Cook the Chicken (or Protein):

- Add the thinly sliced chicken (or your choice of protein) to the skillet. Stir-fry until the chicken is browned on all sides, about 5-7 minutes.

4. Add Coconut Milk and Broth:

- Pour in the coconut milk and chicken broth, stirring until well combined with the curry paste and chicken.

5. Season and Simmer:

- Add fish sauce and brown sugar (or palm sugar) to the skillet. Stir well to combine.
- Bring the curry to a simmer, then reduce the heat to low and let it simmer gently for about 10-15 minutes, stirring occasionally, until the chicken is cooked through and the sauce has thickened slightly.

6. Add Vegetables:

- Add sliced red bell pepper and green beans to the curry. Cook for another 5-7 minutes until the vegetables are tender-crisp.

7. Garnish and Serve:

- Remove the skillet from heat. Taste and adjust the seasoning if needed, adding more fish sauce or sugar as desired.
- Serve hot, garnished with fresh Thai basil leaves if available.
- Enjoy your homemade Panang Curry with steamed jasmine rice or rice noodles.

This Panang Curry recipe yields a deliciously creamy and aromatic dish with a mild heat level, perfect for a satisfying Thai-inspired meal at home. Adjust the spiciness by varying the amount of Panang curry paste used.

Thai Spring Rolls

Ingredients:

For the Spring Rolls:

- 10-12 spring roll wrappers (8-9 inches in diameter)
- 1 cup cooked shrimp, peeled, deveined, and chopped (or substitute with chicken or tofu)
- 1 cup bean sprouts
- 1 cup shredded carrots
- 1 cup shredded cabbage
- 1/2 cup cooked vermicelli noodles (optional)
- 2 tablespoons chopped fresh cilantro
- 2 tablespoons chopped fresh mint
- 2 tablespoons chopped fresh Thai basil (or regular basil)
- Salt and pepper, to taste
- Vegetable oil, for frying

For the Dipping Sauce:

- 1/4 cup soy sauce
- 2 tablespoons rice vinegar
- 1 tablespoon sugar
- 1 clove garlic, minced
- 1/2 teaspoon red pepper flakes (optional, for heat)
- 1 tablespoon chopped peanuts (optional, for garnish)

Instructions:

1. Prepare the Filling:

- In a large bowl, combine chopped shrimp (or chicken/tofu), bean sprouts, shredded carrots, shredded cabbage, cooked vermicelli noodles (if using), cilantro, mint, and Thai basil. Season with salt and pepper to taste. Mix well.

2. Assemble the Spring Rolls:

- Fill a shallow dish with warm water. Working with one spring roll wrapper at a time, dip the wrapper into the water for about 5-10 seconds until it becomes soft and pliable.
- Lay the softened wrapper flat on a clean surface. Place a small amount of the filling mixture (about 2-3 tablespoons) in the center of the wrapper.

3. Roll the Spring Rolls:

- Fold the bottom edge of the wrapper over the filling. Fold in the sides of the wrapper towards the center. Continue to roll the wrapper tightly until the spring roll is sealed. Repeat with remaining wrappers and filling.

4. Fry the Spring Rolls:

- Heat vegetable oil in a deep skillet or wok over medium-high heat until it reaches 350°F (175°C).
- Carefully place the spring rolls seam-side down into the hot oil, in batches to avoid overcrowding. Fry for about 2-3 minutes, turning occasionally, until they are golden brown and crispy.

5. Drain and Serve:

- Remove the spring rolls from the oil using a slotted spoon or tongs. Drain on paper towels to remove excess oil.

6. Make the Dipping Sauce:

- In a small bowl, whisk together soy sauce, rice vinegar, sugar, minced garlic, and red pepper flakes (if using). Adjust seasoning to taste.

7. Serve:

- Serve the Thai Spring Rolls hot and crispy, with the dipping sauce on the side.
- Optionally, garnish with chopped peanuts for added crunch and flavor.

Enjoy your homemade Thai Spring Rolls as a delightful appetizer or snack! They're best served immediately while crispy and hot. Adjust the filling ingredients to suit your preferences and dietary needs.

Pineapple Fried Rice

Ingredients:

- 2 cups cooked jasmine rice (preferably leftover and cooled)
- 1 cup fresh pineapple, diced into small pieces
- 1/2 lb chicken breast or shrimp, diced (optional)
- 2 tablespoons vegetable oil
- 2 cloves garlic, minced
- 1/2 onion, finely chopped
- 1 red bell pepper, diced
- 1/2 cup frozen peas and carrots mix (or diced carrots)
- 2 green onions, thinly sliced
- 2 eggs, lightly beaten
- 2 tablespoons soy sauce
- 1 tablespoon fish sauce
- 1 tablespoon curry powder
- 1 tablespoon brown sugar (optional)
- 1/4 cup roasted cashew nuts or peanuts, chopped (optional)
- Fresh cilantro for garnish
- Lime wedges for serving

Instructions:

1. **Prepare the Ingredients:**
    - If you haven't already, cook the jasmine rice and allow it to cool completely. Leftover rice works best for fried rice as it's less sticky.
    - Dice the pineapple, chicken/shrimp (if using), onion, red bell pepper, and green onions. Prepare the garlic, eggs, and optional cashew nuts or peanuts.
2. **Stir-Fry the Ingredients:**
    - Heat vegetable oil in a large skillet or wok over medium-high heat.
    - Add minced garlic and chopped onion, and stir-fry for about 1-2 minutes until fragrant.
    - If using chicken or shrimp, add it to the skillet and cook until it is almost cooked through.
3. **Add Vegetables and Pineapple:**
    - Push the cooked protein to one side of the skillet. Pour the lightly beaten eggs into the empty space and scramble until just cooked.
    - Add diced red bell pepper, frozen peas and carrots (or diced carrots), and diced pineapple to the skillet. Stir-fry for about 2-3 minutes until the vegetables are tender.
4. **Combine with Rice:**
    - Add the cooked jasmine rice to the skillet. Use a spatula or spoon to break up any clumps of rice and mix everything together evenly.
5. **Season the Fried Rice:**

- Drizzle soy sauce, fish sauce, and curry powder evenly over the rice and vegetable mixture. Stir well to combine.
- Optionally, add brown sugar to balance the flavors. Taste and adjust seasoning as needed.

6. **Finish and Serve:**
   - Remove the skillet from heat. Stir in chopped green onions and optional chopped cashew nuts or peanuts.
   - Garnish with fresh cilantro and serve hot, with lime wedges on the side for squeezing over the rice.

Enjoy your homemade Pineapple Fried Rice! It's a flavorful and satisfying dish that's perfect for a main meal or as a side dish to complement a Thai-inspired spread. Adjust the ingredients and seasoning to suit your taste preferences.

Thai Fish Cakes (Tod Mun Pla)

Ingredients:

- 1 lb white fish fillets (such as tilapia or cod), finely minced or ground
- 2 tablespoons red curry paste
- 1 tablespoon fish sauce
- 1 tablespoon oyster sauce
- 1 tablespoon sugar
- 1 egg
- 2 kaffir lime leaves, finely shredded (optional)
- 1/2 cup green beans, finely chopped
- 1/4 cup finely chopped fresh cilantro
- Vegetable oil, for frying
- Thai sweet chili sauce, for serving
- Cucumber slices and lettuce leaves, for serving

Instructions:

1. **Prepare the Fish Mixture:**
    - In a large bowl, combine minced or ground fish fillets, red curry paste, fish sauce, oyster sauce, sugar, and egg. Mix well until all ingredients are thoroughly combined.
2. **Add Herbs and Vegetables:**
    - Add shredded kaffir lime leaves (if using), chopped green beans, and chopped cilantro to the fish mixture. Mix until evenly distributed.
3. **Shape the Fish Cakes:**
    - Take a small handful of the fish mixture and shape it into a round patty, about 2 inches in diameter and 1/2 inch thick. Repeat until all the mixture is used up. You should get about 12 fish cakes.
4. **Fry the Fish Cakes:**
    - Heat vegetable oil in a large skillet or wok over medium-high heat, enough to cover the bottom of the pan.
    - Carefully place the fish cakes into the hot oil, in batches if necessary to avoid overcrowding. Fry for about 3-4 minutes on each side, or until they are golden brown and cooked through.
5. **Serve:**
    - Remove the fish cakes from the oil and drain on paper towels to remove excess oil.
    - Serve hot with Thai sweet chili sauce for dipping.
    - Optionally, serve with cucumber slices and lettuce leaves as garnish.

Enjoy your homemade Thai Fish Cakes (Tod Mun Pla)! They make a delicious appetizer or snack with a perfect balance of flavors. Adjust the spiciness by varying the amount of red curry paste used.

Khao Soi (Northern Thai Curry Noodles)

Ingredients:

For the Khao Soi Paste:

- 4 dried red chilies, soaked in warm water for 15-20 minutes
- 4 cloves garlic
- 2 shallots, chopped
- 1-inch piece of ginger, peeled and chopped
- 1 tablespoon ground coriander
- 1 tablespoon curry powder
- 1 teaspoon turmeric powder
- 1 tablespoon shrimp paste (optional, for authentic flavor)
- 2 tablespoons vegetable oil

For the Curry:

- 1 lb chicken thighs or chicken breast, thinly sliced (or substitute with beef, pork, or tofu)
- 2 tablespoons vegetable oil
- 1 can (14 oz) coconut milk
- 3 cups chicken broth
- 2 tablespoons soy sauce
- 1 tablespoon fish sauce
- 1 tablespoon brown sugar (or palm sugar)
- Salt, to taste
- 8 oz egg noodles, cooked according to package instructions

For Serving:

- Crispy fried egg noodles (available in Asian markets or homemade)
- Fresh cilantro leaves
- Lime wedges
- Sliced shallots or red onions, thinly sliced
- Pickled mustard greens (optional)

Instructions:

1. Prepare the Khao Soi Paste:

- Drain the soaked dried red chilies and roughly chop them.
- In a food processor or blender, combine the soaked red chilies, garlic, chopped shallots, chopped ginger, ground coriander, curry powder, turmeric powder, and shrimp paste (if using).
- Blend into a smooth paste, adding vegetable oil as needed to facilitate blending.

2. Cook the Chicken:

- Heat vegetable oil in a large pot or Dutch oven over medium-high heat.
- Add the Khao Soi paste to the pot and stir-fry for 1-2 minutes until fragrant.
- Add the sliced chicken to the pot and cook until it is almost cooked through, about 5-7 minutes.

3. Add Coconut Milk and Broth:

- Pour in the coconut milk and chicken broth, stirring until well combined with the Khao Soi paste and chicken.

4. Season the Curry:

- Add soy sauce, fish sauce, and brown sugar (or palm sugar) to the pot. Stir well to combine.
- Taste and adjust seasoning with salt as needed. Bring the curry to a simmer and let it cook for another 10-15 minutes to allow flavors to meld together.

5. Prepare the Noodles:

- Cook the egg noodles according to package instructions until al dente. Drain and set aside.

6. Serve Khao Soi:

- To serve, divide the cooked egg noodles among serving bowls.
- Ladle the hot Khao Soi curry over the noodles.
- Top each bowl with crispy fried egg noodles, fresh cilantro leaves, sliced shallots or red onions, and a wedge of lime.
- Optionally, serve with pickled mustard greens on the side.

Enjoy your homemade Khao Soi! It's a comforting and flavorful dish that captures the essence of Northern Thai cuisine. Adjust the spiciness by varying the amount of dried red chilies used in the Khao Soi paste.

Thai Beef Salad

Ingredients:

For the Beef:

- 1 lb beef steak (such as sirloin or flank steak)
- Salt and pepper, to taste
- Vegetable oil, for grilling

For the Salad:

- 1 cucumber, thinly sliced
- 1 red onion, thinly sliced
- 1 cup cherry tomatoes, halved
- 1/2 cup fresh cilantro leaves
- 1/2 cup fresh mint leaves
- 1/4 cup chopped green onions

For the Dressing:

- 3 tablespoons fish sauce
- 2 tablespoons lime juice
- 1 tablespoon soy sauce
- 1 tablespoon brown sugar (or palm sugar)
- 1-2 Thai bird's eye chilies, finely chopped (adjust to your spice preference)
- 2 cloves garlic, minced

Instructions:

1. Prepare the Beef:

- Season the beef steak with salt and pepper on both sides.
- Heat a grill or grill pan over medium-high heat. Brush the grill with vegetable oil.
- Grill the beef steak for about 3-4 minutes per side, or until it reaches your desired doneness (medium-rare is recommended). Cooking time will vary depending on the thickness of the steak.
- Remove the steak from the grill and let it rest for 5-10 minutes before slicing thinly against the grain.

2. Prepare the Dressing:

- In a small bowl, whisk together fish sauce, lime juice, soy sauce, brown sugar, chopped Thai bird's eye chilies, and minced garlic until the sugar has dissolved. Adjust seasoning to taste, adding more lime juice or fish sauce if needed for balance.

3. Assemble the Salad:

- In a large bowl, combine the sliced cucumber, red onion, cherry tomatoes, cilantro leaves, mint leaves, and chopped green onions.
- Add the sliced grilled beef to the bowl with the salad ingredients.

4. Toss with Dressing:

- Pour the dressing over the salad and grilled beef. Toss gently to combine, ensuring that everything is coated evenly with the dressing.

5. Serve:

- Transfer the Thai Beef Salad to serving plates or bowls.
- Optionally, garnish with additional cilantro leaves and mint leaves on top.
- Serve immediately and enjoy your flavorful Thai Beef Salad!

This Thai Beef Salad is perfect for a light and refreshing meal, packed with bold flavors from the herbs and tangy dressing. Adjust the spice level by adding more or less Thai bird's eye chilies. Serve it as a main dish or as part of a Thai-inspired meal spread.

Pad Kee Mao (Drunken Noodles)

Ingredients:

- 8 oz wide rice noodles
- 2 tablespoons vegetable oil
- 2 cloves garlic, minced
- 1 shallot, thinly sliced
- 1 bell pepper, sliced (red or green)
- 1 cup sliced vegetables (such as broccoli florets, snap peas, or baby corn)
- 1 lb protein of your choice (chicken, beef, shrimp, or tofu), thinly sliced or cubed
- 2-3 Thai bird's eye chilies, minced (adjust to your spice preference)
- 2 tablespoons oyster sauce
- 1 tablespoon soy sauce
- 1 tablespoon fish sauce
- 1 tablespoon dark soy sauce (or sweet soy sauce)
- 1 teaspoon sugar
- Handful of Thai basil leaves
- Fresh cilantro leaves for garnish
- Lime wedges for serving

Instructions:

1. **Prepare the Rice Noodles:**
   - Cook the wide rice noodles according to package instructions until they are al dente. Drain and rinse with cold water to prevent sticking. Set aside.
2. **Stir-Fry the Ingredients:**
   - Heat vegetable oil in a large wok or skillet over medium-high heat.
   - Add minced garlic and sliced shallot. Stir-fry for about 1 minute until fragrant.
3. **Cook the Protein:**
   - Push the garlic and shallot to one side of the wok. Add the sliced protein (chicken, beef, shrimp, or tofu) to the wok. Stir-fry until it is almost cooked through, about 3-4 minutes depending on the protein.
4. **Add Vegetables:**
   - Add sliced bell pepper and other vegetables (like broccoli florets or snap peas) to the wok. Stir-fry for another 2-3 minutes until the vegetables start to soften.
5. **Combine Noodles and Sauce:**
   - Add the cooked rice noodles to the wok. Toss gently with the cooked ingredients to combine.
6. **Make the Sauce:**
   - In a small bowl, mix together oyster sauce, soy sauce, fish sauce, dark soy sauce (or sweet soy sauce), and sugar until well combined.
7. **Add Sauce and Finish:**

- Pour the sauce over the noodles and stir-fry everything together for another 2-3 minutes, ensuring the noodles are evenly coated with the sauce and everything is heated through.

8. **Add Thai Basil and Serve:**
   - Add Thai basil leaves to the wok and toss until they wilt slightly.
   - Remove from heat. Taste and adjust seasoning if needed.
9. **Serve:**
   - Transfer Pad Kee Mao to serving plates or bowls.
   - Garnish with fresh cilantro leaves and serve with lime wedges on the side.

Enjoy your homemade Pad Kee Mao (Drunken Noodles)! It's a deliciously spicy and aromatic dish that's perfect for a satisfying meal. Adjust the level of spiciness by varying the amount of Thai bird's eye chilies used.

Thai Crab Curry

Ingredients:

- 2-3 fresh crabs (cleaned and cracked into pieces, or use crab meat if preferred)
- 2 tablespoons vegetable oil
- 3 cloves garlic, minced
- 1 small onion, thinly sliced
- 1 red bell pepper, sliced
- 1 yellow bell pepper, sliced
- 1 carrot, thinly sliced
- 1 tablespoon yellow curry paste
- 1 can (14 oz) coconut milk
- 1 tablespoon fish sauce
- 1 tablespoon soy sauce
- 1 tablespoon brown sugar (or palm sugar)
- 1 cup chicken broth or seafood broth
- 1 tablespoon lime juice
- Fresh cilantro leaves for garnish

Instructions:

1. **Prepare the Crabs:**
    - If using whole crabs, clean them thoroughly and crack into pieces. If using crab meat, ensure it is picked clean of any shell fragments.
2. **Cooking the Curry:**
    - Heat vegetable oil in a large skillet or wok over medium-high heat.
    - Add minced garlic and thinly sliced onion. Stir-fry for about 1-2 minutes until fragrant.
3. **Add Vegetables:**
    - Add sliced red bell pepper, yellow bell pepper, and thinly sliced carrot to the skillet. Stir-fry for another 2-3 minutes until the vegetables start to soften.
4. **Add Curry Paste and Coconut Milk:**
    - Push the vegetables to the side of the skillet. Add yellow curry paste to the skillet and stir-fry for about 1 minute until fragrant.
    - Pour in coconut milk and stir well to combine with the curry paste and vegetables.
5. **Season the Curry:**
    - Add fish sauce, soy sauce, and brown sugar (or palm sugar) to the skillet. Stir to mix the ingredients together.
6. **Simmer the Curry:**
    - Pour in chicken broth or seafood broth to the skillet. Bring the curry to a simmer and let it cook for about 5 minutes, stirring occasionally.
7. **Add Crab Meat:**
    - Add the cleaned and cracked crab pieces (or crab meat) to the skillet. Stir gently to coat the crab pieces with the curry sauce.

8. **Finish and Serve:**
    - Let the crab curry simmer for another 5-7 minutes, or until the crab is cooked through and heated.
9. **Garnish and Serve:**
    - Remove the skillet from heat. Stir in lime juice.
    - Serve the Thai Crab Curry hot, garnished with fresh cilantro leaves.

Enjoy your homemade Thai Crab Curry with steamed jasmine rice or crusty bread! It's a flavorful and comforting dish that highlights the delicate sweetness of crab meat in a rich coconut curry sauce. Adjust the spiciness by varying the amount of yellow curry paste used.

Thai Chicken Green Curry Fried Rice

Ingredients:

- 2 cups cooked jasmine rice (preferably leftover and cooled)
- 1 lb boneless, skinless chicken thighs or breasts, cut into bite-sized pieces
- 2 tablespoons green curry paste
- 1 can (14 oz) coconut milk
- 1 cup chicken broth or vegetable broth
- 1 red bell pepper, diced
- 1 cup green beans, cut into 1-inch pieces
- 1 carrot, diced
- 4-5 kaffir lime leaves, torn into pieces (optional)
- 2 tablespoons fish sauce
- 1 tablespoon soy sauce
- 1 tablespoon brown sugar (or palm sugar)
- 1 tablespoon vegetable oil
- Fresh Thai basil leaves for garnish (optional)
- Lime wedges for serving

Instructions:

1. **Prepare the Chicken:**
   - Heat vegetable oil in a large skillet or wok over medium-high heat.
   - Add chicken pieces and stir-fry until they are cooked through and lightly browned. Remove from the skillet and set aside.
2. **Make the Green Curry Sauce:**
   - In the same skillet, add green curry paste and cook for 1-2 minutes until fragrant.
   - Pour in coconut milk and chicken broth. Stir well to combine with the curry paste.
3. **Cook the Vegetables:**
   - Add diced red bell pepper, green beans, carrot, and torn kaffir lime leaves (if using) to the skillet. Simmer for about 5 minutes until the vegetables are tender-crisp.
4. **Season the Curry Sauce:**
   - Stir in fish sauce, soy sauce, and brown sugar (or palm sugar) into the curry sauce. Adjust seasoning to taste.
5. **Add Rice and Chicken:**
   - Add cooked jasmine rice to the skillet. Stir-fry for 2-3 minutes, breaking up any clumps of rice and ensuring it's well coated with the curry sauce.
6. **Combine and Finish:**
   - Return the cooked chicken pieces to the skillet. Stir-fry for another 2-3 minutes until everything is heated through and well combined.
7. **Garnish and Serve:**
   - Remove from heat. Garnish with fresh Thai basil leaves (if using).
   - Serve hot, with lime wedges on the side for squeezing over the fried rice.

Enjoy your Thai Chicken Green Curry Fried Rice! It's a delightful combination of creamy green curry flavors with the satisfying texture of fried rice, perfect for a flavorful meal at home. Adjust the spiciness by varying the amount of green curry paste used.

Thai Grilled Chicken (Gai Yang)

Ingredients:

- 4 boneless, skinless chicken thighs or chicken breasts
- **For the Marinade:**
    - 4 cloves garlic, minced
    - 2 stalks lemongrass, finely minced (white part only)
    - 1 tablespoon grated fresh ginger
    - 2 tablespoons soy sauce
    - 2 tablespoons fish sauce
    - 2 tablespoons vegetable oil
    - 2 tablespoons honey or brown sugar
    - 1 tablespoon oyster sauce
    - 1 teaspoon ground coriander
    - 1 teaspoon ground turmeric (or use fresh turmeric if available)
    - 1/2 teaspoon ground white pepper
    - 1/2 teaspoon chili powder (adjust to taste)
    - 1/2 teaspoon salt

Instructions:

1. **Prepare the Marinade:**
    - In a bowl, combine minced garlic, minced lemongrass, grated ginger, soy sauce, fish sauce, vegetable oil, honey or brown sugar, oyster sauce, ground coriander, ground turmeric, ground white pepper, chili powder, and salt. Mix well until the marinade is smooth.
2. **Marinate the Chicken:**
    - Place the chicken thighs or breasts in a shallow dish or resealable plastic bag.
    - Pour the marinade over the chicken, making sure each piece is well coated. Massage the marinade into the chicken to ensure even distribution.
    - Cover the dish or seal the bag, and refrigerate for at least 2 hours, or preferably overnight to allow the flavors to meld.
3. **Grill the Chicken:**
    - Preheat your grill to medium-high heat.
    - Remove the chicken from the marinade, shaking off any excess marinade.
    - Grill the chicken for about 6-8 minutes per side, or until fully cooked and nicely charred with grill marks. The internal temperature should reach 165°F (75°C) for chicken.
4. **Rest and Serve:**
    - Remove the grilled chicken from the grill and let it rest for a few minutes before slicing.
    - Serve the Thai Grilled Chicken (Gai Yang) hot, garnished with fresh cilantro and accompanied by sticky rice and your favorite dipping sauce, such as sweet chili sauce or a spicy Thai dipping sauce.

Enjoy your homemade Thai Grilled Chicken (Gai Yang)! It's flavorful, tender, and pairs wonderfully with fresh herbs and rice. Adjust the spice level to your preference by adding more or less chili powder in the marinade.

Thai Pork Satay

Ingredients:

For the Pork Satay:

- 1 lb pork tenderloin or pork loin, thinly sliced into strips
- Bamboo skewers, soaked in water for 30 minutes (to prevent burning)
- **Marinade:**
    - 3 cloves garlic, minced
    - 1 tablespoon lemongrass, finely minced (white part only)
    - 1 tablespoon grated fresh ginger
    - 2 tablespoons soy sauce
    - 1 tablespoon fish sauce
    - 1 tablespoon vegetable oil
    - 1 tablespoon brown sugar
    - 1 teaspoon ground coriander
    - 1 teaspoon ground cumin
    - 1/2 teaspoon turmeric powder
    - 1/2 teaspoon ground white pepper
- Fresh cilantro leaves, for garnish
- Lime wedges, for serving

For the Peanut Dipping Sauce:

- 1/2 cup creamy peanut butter
- 1/4 cup coconut milk
- 2 tablespoons soy sauce
- 1 tablespoon brown sugar
- 1 tablespoon lime juice
- 1 teaspoon fish sauce (optional)
- 1/2 teaspoon red pepper flakes (optional, for spice)
- Water, as needed to thin out the sauce

Instructions:

1. Prepare the Marinade:

- In a bowl, combine minced garlic, minced lemongrass, grated ginger, soy sauce, fish sauce, vegetable oil, brown sugar, ground coriander, ground cumin, turmeric powder, and ground white pepper. Mix well to form a smooth marinade.

2. Marinate the Pork:

- Place the thinly sliced pork strips into a shallow dish or resealable plastic bag.

- Pour the marinade over the pork, making sure all pieces are evenly coated. Massage the marinade into the pork.
- Cover the dish or seal the bag, and refrigerate for at least 2 hours, or preferably overnight, to allow the flavors to penetrate the meat.

3. Make the Peanut Dipping Sauce:

- In a small saucepan over medium heat, combine peanut butter, coconut milk, soy sauce, brown sugar, lime juice, fish sauce (if using), and red pepper flakes (if using).
- Stir constantly until the mixture is smooth and heated through. If the sauce is too thick, gradually add water to reach your desired consistency. Remove from heat and set aside.

4. Skewer and Grill the Pork:

- Preheat your grill or grill pan over medium-high heat.
- Thread the marinated pork strips onto the soaked bamboo skewers, shaking off any excess marinade.
- Grill the pork skewers for about 3-4 minutes per side, or until the pork is cooked through and nicely charred with grill marks.

5. Serve:

- Arrange the grilled Thai Pork Satay skewers on a serving platter.
- Garnish with fresh cilantro leaves and serve with lime wedges and the prepared Peanut Dipping Sauce on the side.

Enjoy your homemade Thai Pork Satay! It's a delicious appetizer or main dish that's perfect for sharing with friends and family. Adjust the spice level of the Peanut Dipping Sauce according to your preference by adding more or less red pepper flakes.

Stir-Fried Morning Glory (Pad Pak Boong Fai Daeng)

Ingredients:

- 1 bunch of morning glory (water spinach), about 1 lb
- 2-3 cloves garlic, minced
- 2-3 Thai bird's eye chilies, minced (adjust to taste)
- 1 tablespoon oyster sauce
- 1 tablespoon soy sauce
- 1 teaspoon fish sauce
- 1 teaspoon sugar
- 1 tablespoon vegetable oil
- 1/4 cup water
- Optional: sliced red bell pepper for color

Instructions:

1. **Prepare the Morning Glory:**
    - Rinse the morning glory thoroughly under cold water. Trim off any tough ends and cut into 2-inch pieces. Separate the stems and leaves if they are large.
2. **Make the Stir-Fry Sauce:**
    - In a small bowl, mix together oyster sauce, soy sauce, fish sauce, and sugar until well combined. Set aside.
3. **Stir-Fry the Morning Glory:**
    - Heat vegetable oil in a large wok or skillet over medium-high heat.
    - Add minced garlic and Thai bird's eye chilies. Stir-fry for about 30 seconds until fragrant.
4. **Add Morning Glory:**
    - Add the prepared morning glory to the wok. Stir-fry for about 1-2 minutes, using tongs or a spatula to toss the vegetables continuously.
5. **Add Sauce and Water:**
    - Pour the prepared stir-fry sauce over the morning glory. Add 1/4 cup of water to the wok.
    - Continue stir-frying for another 2-3 minutes, or until the morning glory is wilted and tender, and the sauce has reduced slightly. If using, add sliced red bell pepper for color and additional crunch.
6. **Serve:**
    - Remove from heat and transfer Stir-Fried Morning Glory to a serving dish.
    - Serve hot as a side dish with steamed jasmine rice or as part of a Thai meal spread.

Enjoy your homemade Stir-Fried Morning Glory (Pad Pak Boong Fai Daeng)! It's a quick and delicious way to enjoy fresh greens with bold Thai flavors. Adjust the spiciness by varying the amount of Thai bird's eye chilies used.

Thai Shrimp Cakes

Ingredients:

- 1 lb shrimp, peeled and deveined
- 1 egg
- 3 cloves garlic, minced
- 1 tablespoon red curry paste
- 1 tablespoon fish sauce
- 1 tablespoon soy sauce
- 1 tablespoon brown sugar
- 1/2 teaspoon ground white pepper
- 1/2 cup green beans, finely chopped
- 1/4 cup fresh cilantro, chopped
- 1/4 cup fresh Thai basil leaves, chopped (optional)
- Vegetable oil, for frying

For Serving:

- Sweet chili sauce or Thai dipping sauce
- Cucumber slices
- Lettuce leaves

Instructions:

1. **Prepare the Shrimp:**
   - In a food processor, pulse the shrimp until finely minced, but not completely smooth. Alternatively, finely chop the shrimp with a knife.
2. **Make the Shrimp Cake Mixture:**
   - In a large bowl, combine the minced shrimp, egg, minced garlic, red curry paste, fish sauce, soy sauce, brown sugar, and ground white pepper. Mix well until all ingredients are thoroughly combined.
3. **Add Vegetables and Herbs:**
   - Fold in the chopped green beans, chopped cilantro, and chopped Thai basil leaves (if using) into the shrimp mixture. Mix until evenly distributed.
4. **Shape the Shrimp Cakes:**
   - Take a small handful of the shrimp mixture and shape it into a small patty, about 2 inches in diameter and 1/2 inch thick. Repeat until all the mixture is used up. You should get about 12 shrimp cakes.
5. **Fry the Shrimp Cakes:**
   - Heat vegetable oil in a large skillet or frying pan over medium-high heat.
   - Carefully place the shrimp cakes into the hot oil, in batches if necessary to avoid overcrowding. Fry for about 3-4 minutes on each side, or until they are golden brown and cooked through.
6. **Serve:**

- Remove the shrimp cakes from the oil and drain on paper towels to remove excess oil.
- Serve hot with sweet chili sauce or Thai dipping sauce for dipping.
- Optionally, serve with cucumber slices and lettuce leaves as garnish.

Enjoy your homemade Thai Shrimp Cakes (Tod Mun Goong)! They make a delightful appetizer or snack with a perfect balance of flavors and textures. Adjust the spiciness by varying the amount of red curry paste used.

Thai Pumpkin Curry

Ingredients:

- 2 cups pumpkin, peeled and cubed
- 1 can (14 oz) coconut milk
- 1 onion, thinly sliced
- 2 cloves garlic, minced
- 1 red bell pepper, sliced
- 1-2 tablespoons red curry paste (adjust to taste)
- 1 tablespoon vegetable oil
- 1 tablespoon soy sauce
- 1 tablespoon brown sugar (optional)
- 1 tablespoon lime juice
- Fresh cilantro leaves, for garnish
- Salt to taste
- Cooked rice, for serving

Instructions:

1. **Prepare the Pumpkin:**
   - Peel the pumpkin and remove seeds. Cut into bite-sized cubes.
2. **Sauté Vegetables:**
   - Heat vegetable oil in a large pan or wok over medium heat.
   - Add sliced onion and minced garlic. Sauté until onions are translucent and garlic is fragrant.
3. **Add Curry Paste:**
   - Add red curry paste to the pan. Stir and cook for about 1 minute until fragrant.
4. **Cook Pumpkin:**
   - Add the cubed pumpkin to the pan. Stir to coat with the curry paste mixture.
5. **Simmer:**
   - Pour in the coconut milk and stir well. Bring to a simmer.
6. **Add Bell Pepper:**
   - Add sliced red bell pepper to the pan. Stir to combine.
7. **Seasoning:**
   - Add soy sauce, brown sugar (if using), and lime juice to the curry. Stir well. Taste and adjust seasoning as needed, adding salt if desired.
8. **Simmer Until Pumpkin is Tender:**
   - Reduce heat to medium-low and let the curry simmer gently for about 15-20 minutes, or until the pumpkin is tender and cooked through.
9. **Serve:**
   - Once the pumpkin is cooked, remove from heat. Serve the Thai pumpkin curry hot, garnished with fresh cilantro leaves and accompanied by cooked rice.

Enjoy your delicious Thai Pumpkin Curry!

Thai Basil Eggplant

Ingredients:

- 2 medium-sized eggplants, cut into cubes
- 3 tablespoons vegetable oil
- 4 cloves garlic, minced
- 1 red chili, thinly sliced (optional, for spice)
- 1 bell pepper, thinly sliced
- 1 onion, thinly sliced
- 1 cup Thai basil leaves
- 2 tablespoons soy sauce
- 1 tablespoon oyster sauce (optional)
- 1 tablespoon fish sauce (or soy sauce for vegetarian)
- 1 teaspoon sugar
- 1/2 cup water
- Cooked rice, for serving

Instructions:

1. **Prepare Eggplant:**
    - Cut the eggplants into cubes. If using large eggplants, you can optionally salt them and let them sit for 10-15 minutes to draw out bitterness, then rinse and pat dry.
2. **Heat Oil:**
    - Heat vegetable oil in a large pan or wok over medium-high heat.
3. **Cook Garlic and Chili:**
    - Add minced garlic and sliced red chili (if using) to the pan. Stir-fry for about 30 seconds until fragrant.
4. **Add Eggplant:**
    - Add the cubed eggplant to the pan. Stir-fry for 3-4 minutes until the eggplant starts to soften.
5. **Add Bell Pepper and Onion:**
    - Add sliced bell pepper and onion to the pan. Continue stir-frying for another 2-3 minutes until vegetables are tender-crisp.
6. **Sauce Mixture:**
    - In a small bowl, mix together soy sauce, oyster sauce (if using), fish sauce (or more soy sauce for vegetarian), and sugar.
7. **Combine Sauce:**
    - Pour the sauce mixture over the vegetables in the pan. Stir well to coat evenly.
8. **Add Thai Basil:**
    - Tear the Thai basil leaves roughly and add them to the pan. Stir-fry for another minute until the basil is wilted and aromatic.
9. **Adjust Consistency:**

- If the dish looks too dry, add 1/2 cup of water to create a bit of sauce. Stir well to combine.
10. **Serve:**
    - Once everything is cooked through and well combined, remove from heat. Serve the Thai Basil Eggplant hot, accompanied by cooked rice.

Enjoy this flavorful and aromatic Thai Basil Eggplant as a delicious main dish!

Thai Glass Noodle Salad (Yum Woon Sen)

Ingredients:

- 100g glass noodles (bean thread noodles)
- 1 cup cooked shrimp, peeled and deveined (optional)
- 1 cup cooked chicken breast, shredded (optional)
- 1 cup cherry tomatoes, halved
- 1/2 cup cucumber, thinly sliced
- 1/4 cup red onion, thinly sliced
- 1/4 cup cilantro leaves, chopped
- 1/4 cup mint leaves, chopped
- 1/4 cup roasted peanuts, chopped (optional, for garnish)

For the Dressing:

- 3 tablespoons lime juice
- 2 tablespoons fish sauce (or soy sauce for vegetarian)
- 1 tablespoon sugar
- 1-2 red chilies, finely chopped (adjust to taste)
- 2 cloves garlic, minced

Instructions:

1. **Prepare Glass Noodles:**
   - Bring a pot of water to a boil. Add the glass noodles and cook according to package instructions (usually about 5-7 minutes) until noodles are tender but still firm. Drain and rinse under cold water to stop cooking. Set aside.
2. **Prepare Dressing:**
   - In a small bowl, whisk together lime juice, fish sauce (or soy sauce), sugar, chopped red chilies, and minced garlic. Adjust seasoning to taste. Set aside.
3. **Assemble Salad:**
   - In a large mixing bowl, combine the cooked glass noodles, cooked shrimp (if using), cooked chicken (if using), cherry tomatoes, cucumber, red onion, cilantro, and mint leaves.
4. **Add Dressing:**
   - Pour the prepared dressing over the salad ingredients in the bowl. Toss gently to combine, ensuring the noodles and vegetables are evenly coated with the dressing.
5. **Serve:**
   - Transfer the Thai Glass Noodle Salad to a serving platter or individual plates. Garnish with chopped roasted peanuts (if using).
6. **Enjoy:**

- - Serve immediately and enjoy this refreshing and tangy Thai salad as a light and satisfying meal.

This Thai Glass Noodle Salad (Yum Woon Sen) is perfect for a hot summer day or as a side dish to complement a main meal. Adjust the spiciness and ingredients according to your preference for a personalized experience!

Thai Cucumber Salad

Ingredients:

- 2 medium cucumbers, thinly sliced
- 1/4 cup red onion, thinly sliced
- 1-2 red chilies, thinly sliced (adjust to taste)
- 1/4 cup roasted peanuts, roughly chopped (optional, for garnish)
- 1/4 cup fresh cilantro leaves, chopped (for garnish)

For the Dressing:

- 3 tablespoons rice vinegar
- 2 tablespoons lime juice
- 2 tablespoons fish sauce (or soy sauce for vegetarian)
- 1 tablespoon sugar
- 1 clove garlic, minced
- 1/2 teaspoon salt, or to taste

Instructions:

1. **Prepare Cucumbers and Onions:**
   - Thinly slice the cucumbers and red onion. You can use a mandoline slicer or a sharp knife for thin slices. Place them in a large bowl.
2. **Prepare Dressing:**
   - In a small bowl, whisk together rice vinegar, lime juice, fish sauce (or soy sauce), sugar, minced garlic, and salt until the sugar and salt are dissolved.
3. **Combine Salad:**
   - Pour the dressing over the sliced cucumbers and onions in the bowl. Toss gently to coat evenly.
4. **Add Chilies (Optional):**
   - If using red chilies, add them to the salad according to your preferred level of spiciness. Toss again to combine.
5. **Chill (Optional):**
   - You can chill the salad in the refrigerator for about 15-30 minutes before serving to allow the flavors to meld together.
6. **Garnish and Serve:**
   - Before serving, garnish the Thai Cucumber Salad with chopped roasted peanuts (if using) and fresh cilantro leaves.
7. **Enjoy:**
   - Serve the salad chilled or at room temperature as a refreshing side dish or appetizer.

This Thai Cucumber Salad is perfect for balancing out spicy dishes or as a light and refreshing addition to any meal. Adjust the sweetness, sourness, and spiciness of the dressing to suit your taste preferences.

Thai Coconut Soup (Tom Kha)

Ingredients:

- 1 can (14 oz) coconut milk
- 2 cups chicken broth or vegetable broth
- 1 lemongrass stalk, bruised and cut into 2-inch pieces
- 3-4 slices galangal or ginger (about 1-inch each), thinly sliced
- 2-3 kaffir lime leaves, torn or finely sliced
- 1-2 red chilies, thinly sliced (adjust to taste)
- 1 cup mushrooms (such as straw mushrooms or button mushrooms), sliced
- 1 medium tomato, cut into wedges
- 1 small onion, thinly sliced
- 1 lb chicken breast or shrimp, sliced (optional)
- 2 tablespoons fish sauce (or soy sauce for vegetarian)
- 1 tablespoon palm sugar or brown sugar
- 2 tablespoons lime juice
- Fresh cilantro leaves, for garnish
- Fresh Thai basil leaves, for garnish (optional)

Instructions:

1. **Prepare the Soup Base:**
   - In a large pot, combine coconut milk and chicken broth (or vegetable broth) over medium heat. Stir to mix well.
2. **Infuse Flavors:**
   - Add lemongrass stalk pieces, sliced galangal or ginger, torn kaffir lime leaves, and sliced red chilies to the pot. Let it simmer gently for about 5-7 minutes to allow the flavors to infuse into the broth.
3. **Add Protein and Vegetables:**
   - If using chicken or shrimp, add them to the pot and cook until they are almost cooked through.
4. **Add Mushrooms and Tomatoes:**
   - Add sliced mushrooms and tomato wedges to the pot. Continue simmering until the mushrooms are tender and the protein is fully cooked.
5. **Season the Soup:**
   - Stir in fish sauce (or soy sauce) and palm sugar (or brown sugar) to the soup. Adjust the seasoning to taste.
6. **Finish with Lime Juice:**
   - Remove the pot from heat and stir in lime juice. Taste and adjust the sourness and saltiness with more lime juice or fish sauce if needed.
7. **Serve:**
   - Ladle the Tom Kha soup into bowls. Garnish with fresh cilantro leaves and Thai basil leaves (if using).

8. **Enjoy:**
    - Serve the Thai Coconut Soup (Tom Kha) hot as a comforting appetizer or main dish. Enjoy its aromatic flavors!

This soup is a wonderful balance of creamy coconut milk, tangy lime juice, aromatic herbs, and savory broth. Adjust the spiciness with more or fewer red chilies according to your preference.

Thai Fried Chicken

Ingredients:

- 1 lb chicken wings or drumsticks
- 3-4 cloves garlic, minced
- 1 tsp white peppercorns, crushed
- 1 tsp coriander seeds, crushed
- 1/2 tsp salt
- 1/2 tsp sugar
- 1 tbsp oyster sauce
- 1 tbsp soy sauce
- 1 tbsp fish sauce
- 1/2 cup all-purpose flour
- Oil for frying

Instructions:

1. **Prepare the Chicken:**
    - Clean and pat dry the chicken pieces.
    - In a bowl, combine minced garlic, crushed white peppercorns, crushed coriander seeds, salt, sugar, oyster sauce, soy sauce, and fish sauce. Mix well.
    - Add the chicken pieces to the marinade, making sure they are well coated. Marinate for at least 1 hour, or overnight in the refrigerator for more flavor.
2. **Coat the Chicken:**
    - Heat oil in a deep fryer or a heavy-bottomed pot to 350°F (175°C).
    - Place all-purpose flour in a shallow dish.
    - Remove each chicken piece from the marinade, allowing excess marinade to drip off.
    - Coat each piece with flour, shaking off any excess.
3. **Fry the Chicken:**
    - Carefully place the chicken pieces in the hot oil, a few at a time, making sure not to overcrowd the pot.
    - Fry until golden brown and crispy, about 8-10 minutes for drumsticks and slightly less for wings.
    - Remove chicken from oil and drain on paper towels. Let it rest for a few minutes before serving.
4. **Serve:**
    - Serve Thai Fried Chicken hot, garnished with fresh cilantro leaves and lime wedges on the side.
    - Enjoy with sticky rice, Thai sweet chili sauce, or your favorite dipping sauce.

Thai Fried Chicken is crispy on the outside and tender on the inside, with a delicious blend of savory, salty, and slightly sweet flavors. It's a delightful dish that pairs well with a variety of Thai sides and sauces.

Thai Sweet Chili Sauce

Ingredients:

- 1/2 cup water
- 1/2 cup rice vinegar
- 1/2 cup sugar
- 3-4 cloves garlic, minced
- 1-2 red chili peppers, finely chopped (adjust to taste)
- 1 tbsp cornstarch
- 2 tbsp water

Instructions:

1. **Prepare the Sauce:**
   - In a small saucepan, combine water, rice vinegar, and sugar. Heat over medium heat, stirring until sugar dissolves.
2. **Add Flavorings:**
   - Stir in minced garlic and chopped red chili peppers. Adjust the amount of chili peppers according to your desired level of spiciness.
3. **Thicken the Sauce:**
   - In a small bowl, mix cornstarch with 2 tablespoons of water to create a slurry.
   - Slowly pour the cornstarch slurry into the saucepan, stirring continuously to prevent lumps.
4. **Simmer and Thicken:**
   - Bring the mixture to a boil, then reduce the heat and simmer for 5-7 minutes, or until the sauce thickens to your desired consistency. Stir occasionally.
5. **Cool and Store:**
   - Remove from heat and let the sauce cool completely. It will continue to thicken as it cools.
   - Transfer the sweet chili sauce to a jar or bottle and store in the refrigerator.

Tips:

- **Adjust Spiciness:** You can adjust the spiciness of the sauce by varying the amount of red chili peppers used. For a milder sauce, use less chili; for spicier, add more.
- **Consistency:** The sauce should have a smooth and slightly thick consistency once cooled. If it becomes too thick after cooling, you can thin it out with a little water.
- **Usage:** Thai Sweet Chili Sauce can be used as a dipping sauce for fried foods like chicken wings or spring rolls. It also works well as a glaze for grilled meats or seafood.

Homemade Thai Sweet Chili Sauce is fresher and often tastier than store-bought versions, and it allows you to customize the spiciness and sweetness to your liking. Enjoy experimenting with this delicious Thai condiment!

Thai Garlic Shrimp

Ingredients:

- 1 lb large shrimp, peeled and deveined
- 5-6 cloves garlic, minced
- 1/2 cup fresh cilantro leaves, chopped
- 2 tbsp oyster sauce
- 1 tbsp soy sauce
- 1 tbsp fish sauce
- 1 tbsp sugar
- 1/4 tsp ground white pepper
- 2 tbsp vegetable oil
- Fresh cilantro leaves for garnish
- Lime wedges for serving

Instructions:

1. **Prepare the Shrimp:**
   - If not already done, peel and devein the shrimp. Pat them dry with paper towels.
2. **Make the Sauce:**
   - In a small bowl, mix together oyster sauce, soy sauce, fish sauce, sugar, and ground white pepper. Set aside.
3. **Cooking the Shrimp:**
   - Heat vegetable oil in a large skillet or wok over medium-high heat.
   - Add minced garlic to the pan and stir-fry for about 30 seconds, or until fragrant and lightly golden.
4. **Add Shrimp:**
   - Add the shrimp to the skillet in a single layer. Cook for 1-2 minutes on each side, until they turn pink and opaque.
5. **Add Sauce:**
   - Pour the prepared sauce over the shrimp. Stir-fry for another minute or until the shrimp are well-coated and the sauce thickens slightly.
6. **Finish and Serve:**
   - Remove from heat and stir in chopped cilantro leaves.
   - Transfer to a serving dish and garnish with additional cilantro leaves.
   - Serve hot with lime wedges on the side.

Tips:

- **Shrimp Size:** Use large shrimp for this dish, as they are more substantial and hold up well to stir-frying.
- **Garlic:** Adjust the amount of garlic to your preference. It should be fragrant but not overpowering.

- **Customization:** You can add sliced chili peppers for heat or vegetables like bell peppers or snap peas for added crunch and flavor.

Thai Garlic Shrimp is best served immediately, accompanied by steamed rice or noodles. The combination of garlic, oyster sauce, and fish sauce creates a delicious umami-packed sauce that coats the shrimp beautifully. Enjoy this authentic Thai dish at home!

Thai Basil Fried Rice

Ingredients:

- 2 cups cooked jasmine rice (preferably cooled)
- 2 tablespoons oil (vegetable or sesame oil)
- 3 cloves garlic, minced
- 1-2 Thai chilies, finely chopped (adjust to your spice preference)
- 1 small onion, finely chopped
- 1 bell pepper, diced (any color)
- 1 cup mixed vegetables (like peas, carrots, corn)
- 1 tablespoon soy sauce
- 1 tablespoon oyster sauce (optional)
- 1 teaspoon fish sauce (optional)
- 1 teaspoon sugar
- 1 cup Thai basil leaves, loosely packed
- Optional protein: cooked chicken, shrimp, tofu, or egg (as desired)
- Lime wedges and extra Thai basil leaves for garnish

Instructions:

1. **Prepare the Rice:**
    - If you haven't already, cook the jasmine rice according to package instructions and let it cool. Day-old rice works best for fried rice as it's drier.
2. **Heat Oil:**
    - Heat the oil in a large pan or wok over medium-high heat.
3. **Sauté Aromatics:**
    - Add minced garlic and chopped Thai chilies to the pan. Sauté for about 30 seconds until fragrant.
4. **Add Vegetables:**
    - Add chopped onion, diced bell pepper, and mixed vegetables to the pan. Stir-fry for 2-3 minutes until the vegetables are tender-crisp.
5. **Stir in Rice:**
    - Add the cooked jasmine rice to the pan. Break up any clumps and stir-fry for a few minutes to heat through.
6. **Seasoning:**
    - Drizzle soy sauce, oyster sauce (if using), fish sauce (if using), and sprinkle sugar over the rice. Stir well to combine and evenly distribute the sauces.
7. **Add Basil:**
    - Tear the Thai basil leaves roughly and add them to the pan. Stir-fry for another minute until the basil is wilted and aromatic.
8. **Optional Protein:**
    - If you're adding cooked protein (chicken, shrimp, tofu, or scrambled egg), this is the time to stir it into the rice.

9. **Taste and Adjust:**
    - Taste the fried rice and adjust seasoning if needed. You can add more soy sauce or fish sauce according to your preference.
10. **Serve:**
    - Serve the Thai Basil Fried Rice hot, garnished with extra Thai basil leaves and lime wedges on the side.

Enjoy your delicious Thai Basil Fried Rice!

Thai BBQ Pork (Moo Ping)

Ingredients:

- 1 lb pork tenderloin or pork shoulder, thinly sliced into strips
- 2 tablespoons oyster sauce
- 2 tablespoons soy sauce
- 1 tablespoon fish sauce
- 1 tablespoon palm sugar or brown sugar
- 1 tablespoon vegetable oil
- 1 teaspoon ground white pepper
- Bamboo skewers, soaked in water (if using wooden skewers)
- Optional: Thai sweet chili sauce or spicy dipping sauce, for serving

Instructions:

1. **Marinate the Pork:**
   - In a bowl, combine oyster sauce, soy sauce, fish sauce, palm sugar (or brown sugar), vegetable oil, and ground white pepper. Mix well until the sugar is dissolved.
   - Add the thinly sliced pork to the marinade, ensuring all pieces are coated evenly. Marinate for at least 30 minutes to allow the flavors to penetrate the meat.
2. **Skewer the Pork:**
   - Thread the marinated pork strips onto bamboo skewers (pre-soaked in water to prevent burning) or metal skewers.
3. **Grill or Cook:**
   - Heat a grill pan, outdoor grill, or a large skillet over medium-high heat.
   - Grill the skewers for about 3-4 minutes on each side, or until the pork is cooked through and nicely caramelized with grill marks. Baste with any remaining marinade while grilling for extra flavor.
4. **Serve:**
   - Remove the skewers from the grill and let them rest for a few minutes.
   - Serve Moo Ping hot, either as a snack or with steamed rice and a side of Thai sweet chili sauce or spicy dipping sauce.
5. **Enjoy:**
   - Enjoy the Thai BBQ Pork skewers (Moo Ping) as a delicious appetizer or main dish with rice and your favorite Thai condiments.

Moo Ping is traditionally enjoyed as street food in Thailand, but with this recipe, you can recreate the authentic flavors at home!

Thai Stir-Fried Vegetables

Ingredients:

- Assorted vegetables (such as bell peppers, broccoli, carrots, snow peas, baby corn, mushrooms, etc.), sliced or chopped into bite-sized pieces
- 2-3 cloves garlic, minced
- 1 small onion, thinly sliced
- 1-2 fresh red or green chilies, sliced (optional, for heat)
- 2 tablespoons vegetable oil
- 2 tablespoons oyster sauce (for a non-vegetarian version) or soy sauce (for a vegetarian version)
- 1 tablespoon soy sauce
- 1 teaspoon sugar
- A handful of fresh basil leaves (Thai basil is ideal, but Italian basil works too)
- Salt and pepper to taste

Instructions:

1. **Prepare the Vegetables:**
   - Wash and chop all the vegetables into similar-sized pieces so they cook evenly.
2. **Heat the Wok or Pan:**
   - Heat the vegetable oil in a wok or large skillet over medium-high heat.
3. **Stir-Fry:**
   - Add the minced garlic and sliced onion to the hot oil. Stir-fry for about 1 minute until fragrant.
4. **Add Vegetables:**
   - Add the vegetables that take longer to cook first, such as carrots and broccoli. Stir-fry for 2-3 minutes until they start to soften.
5. **Add Sauce:**
   - Push the vegetables to the side of the wok and add the oyster sauce (or soy sauce), soy sauce, and sugar to the center. Stir to combine the sauces.
6. **Combine and Cook:**
   - Mix the sauce with the vegetables and continue to stir-fry for another 2-3 minutes, or until all vegetables are tender-crisp. Adjust seasoning with salt and pepper to taste.
7. **Add Basil Leaves:**
   - Just before removing from heat, tear the fresh basil leaves and toss them into the stir-fry. Stir for another 30 seconds until the basil leaves wilt slightly.
8. **Serve:**
   - Transfer the stir-fried vegetables to a serving dish and serve hot as a side dish or over steamed rice as a main course.

Tips:

- **Vegetable Variations:** Feel free to customize with your favorite vegetables. Thai cuisine often includes vegetables like baby corn, Thai eggplant, and bamboo shoots.
- **Heat Level:** Adjust the amount of chili peppers to your preference for spiciness.
- **Serving Suggestion:** Serve with jasmine rice or brown rice for a complete meal.

Enjoy your Thai Stir-Fried Vegetables! It's a great way to incorporate a variety of colorful veggies into your diet while savoring Thai flavors.

Thai Crab Fried Rice

Ingredients:

- 2 cups cooked jasmine rice (preferably day-old and chilled)
- 200g crab meat (fresh or canned)
- 2 eggs, lightly beaten
- 1 small onion, finely chopped
- 3 cloves garlic, minced
- 1 red chili, thinly sliced (optional for spice)
- 1 cup mixed vegetables (carrots, peas, bell peppers)
- 2 tablespoons soy sauce
- 1 tablespoon fish sauce
- 1 tablespoon oyster sauce
- 1 tablespoon vegetable oil
- Spring onions (scallions) for garnish
- Fresh cilantro for garnish
- Lime wedges for serving

Instructions:

1. **Prepare Ingredients:**
    - If using fresh crab meat, pick through it to remove any shells or cartilage. If using canned crab meat, drain and set aside.
    - Chop the onion, garlic, and red chili. Prepare the mixed vegetables.
2. **Stir-Fry:**
    - Heat the vegetable oil in a large skillet or wok over medium-high heat. Add the minced garlic and chopped onion. Stir-fry for about 1-2 minutes until fragrant and translucent.
3. **Cook Eggs:**
    - Push the garlic and onion to the side of the pan. Pour the beaten eggs into the empty space and scramble until just set.
4. **Add Vegetables and Crab:**
    - Add the mixed vegetables to the skillet. Stir-fry for another 2-3 minutes until the vegetables are tender-crisp.
    - Add the crab meat to the skillet. Gently stir to combine with the vegetables and eggs.
5. **Add Rice:**
    - Add the chilled jasmine rice to the skillet. Use a spatula to break up any clumps and mix well with the other ingredients.
6. **Seasoning:**
    - Drizzle the soy sauce, fish sauce, and oyster sauce over the rice. Stir-fry for another 3-4 minutes, ensuring everything is well combined and heated through.
7. **Final Touches:**

- Taste and adjust seasoning if needed. Add more soy sauce or fish sauce according to your taste preference.
- Remove from heat. Garnish with sliced spring onions (scallions) and fresh cilantro.

8. **Serve:**
    - Serve hot, garnished with lime wedges on the side for an extra burst of freshness.

Enjoy your delicious Thai Crab Fried Rice!

Thai Cashew Chicken

Ingredients:

- 2 boneless, skinless chicken breasts, cut into bite-sized pieces
- 1/2 cup roasted cashew nuts
- 1 bell pepper (any color), cut into strips
- 1 onion, sliced
- 3 cloves garlic, minced
- 1-inch piece of ginger, minced
- 2-3 green onions (scallions), chopped (separate white and green parts)
- 1/2 cup chicken broth or water
- 2 tablespoons soy sauce
- 1 tablespoon oyster sauce
- 1 tablespoon fish sauce
- 1 tablespoon sugar
- 1 tablespoon cornstarch mixed with 2 tablespoons water (optional, for thickening)
- Vegetable oil for cooking
- Fresh cilantro for garnish
- Cooked jasmine rice, to serve

Instructions:

1. **Prepare Ingredients:**
    - Cut the chicken breasts into bite-sized pieces.
    - Slice the bell pepper and onion into strips.
    - Mince the garlic and ginger. Chop the green onions, separating the white and green parts.
    - Roast the cashew nuts in a dry pan over medium heat until lightly golden and fragrant. Set aside.
2. **Marinate Chicken:**
    - In a bowl, combine the chicken pieces with 1 tablespoon soy sauce and 1 tablespoon cornstarch. Mix well and let it marinate for about 15-20 minutes.
3. **Stir-Fry Chicken:**
    - Heat 1 tablespoon of vegetable oil in a large skillet or wok over medium-high heat. Add the marinated chicken pieces and stir-fry until they are cooked through and slightly browned. Remove from the skillet and set aside.
4. **Cook Vegetables:**
    - In the same skillet, add another tablespoon of oil if needed. Add the minced garlic, ginger, and the white parts of the green onions. Stir-fry for about 1 minute until fragrant.
    - Add the sliced bell pepper and onion to the skillet. Stir-fry for 2-3 minutes until they are tender-crisp.
5. **Combine Sauce:**

- In a small bowl, mix together the chicken broth (or water), oyster sauce, fish sauce, and sugar. Pour this sauce mixture into the skillet with the vegetables. Stir well to combine.

6. **Add Chicken and Cashews:**
   - Return the cooked chicken pieces to the skillet. Stir to coat everything evenly with the sauce.

7. **Thicken Sauce (if using):**
   - If you prefer a thicker sauce, stir in the cornstarch mixture (1 tablespoon cornstarch mixed with 2 tablespoons water). Cook for another minute until the sauce has thickened slightly.

8. **Finish and Serve:**
   - Add the roasted cashew nuts to the skillet. Stir to combine.
   - Taste and adjust seasoning if needed, adding more soy sauce or sugar according to your preference.
   - Remove from heat and garnish with the green parts of the chopped green onions and fresh cilantro.

9. **Serve:**
   - Serve hot over cooked jasmine rice.

Enjoy your delicious Thai Cashew Chicken! It pairs wonderfully with jasmine rice and makes for a satisfying meal.

Thai Green Papaya Salad (Som Tum)

Ingredients:

- 1 small green papaya (about 2 cups shredded)
- 2-3 cloves garlic, minced
- 1-2 Thai bird's eye chilies, minced (adjust to spice preference)
- 2 tablespoons roasted peanuts, roughly chopped
- 1-2 tablespoons dried shrimp (optional)
- 1-2 tablespoons palm sugar or brown sugar (adjust to taste)
- 2 tablespoons fish sauce
- 2 tablespoons lime juice (adjust to taste)
- 1 cup cherry tomatoes, halved
- 1 cup long beans or green beans, cut into 1-inch pieces
- Carrots, shredded (optional, for added color and crunch)
- Fresh cilantro leaves for garnish
- Fresh lettuce leaves for serving (optional)

Instructions:

1. **Prepare Papaya:**
   - Peel the green papaya and cut it in half. Remove the seeds. Using a julienne peeler or a grater, shred the papaya into thin strips. Place shredded papaya in a large mixing bowl.
2. **Make Dressing:**
   - In a mortar and pestle, pound the minced garlic and Thai chilies together to release their flavors. You can also use a small food processor for this step.
   - Add palm sugar (or brown sugar), fish sauce, and lime juice to the mortar or processor. Mix until the sugar dissolves and the ingredients are well combined.
3. **Combine Salad:**
   - Add the prepared dressing to the shredded papaya in the mixing bowl. Use a spoon or tongs to toss and coat the papaya thoroughly with the dressing.
4. **Add Vegetables and Nuts:**
   - Add cherry tomatoes, long beans (or green beans), and shredded carrots (if using) to the bowl. Toss everything together gently.
5. **Adjust Seasoning:**
   - Taste the salad and adjust the seasoning as needed. You can add more fish sauce for saltiness, more lime juice for tanginess, or more sugar if you prefer it sweeter.
6. **Add Peanuts and Dried Shrimp:**
   - Sprinkle chopped roasted peanuts and dried shrimp (if using) over the salad. Toss lightly to mix them in.
7. **Serve:**

- Transfer the salad to a serving plate lined with fresh lettuce leaves (optional) for presentation.
- Garnish with fresh cilantro leaves on top.
8. **Enjoy:**
   - Serve immediately as a refreshing appetizer or side dish with steamed rice or grilled meats.

Som Tum is best enjoyed fresh and immediately after preparation to retain its crunchiness and vibrant flavors. Adjust the level of spiciness and sweetness according to your taste preferences for a perfect Thai Green Papaya Salad experience!

Thai Peanut Sauce

Ingredients:

- 1/2 cup creamy peanut butter
- 1/4 cup water (adjust for desired consistency)
- 2 tablespoons soy sauce (or tamari for gluten-free)
- 2 tablespoons lime juice
- 1 tablespoon brown sugar or honey (adjust to taste)
- 1 tablespoon sriracha sauce (adjust to spice preference)
- 1 clove garlic, minced
- 1 teaspoon grated ginger
- Optional: 1 tablespoon coconut milk (for creaminess)

Instructions:

1. **Prepare Peanut Butter Mixture:**
    - In a mixing bowl, combine creamy peanut butter, water, soy sauce, lime juice, brown sugar (or honey), sriracha sauce, minced garlic, and grated ginger.
2. **Mix Thoroughly:**
    - Whisk or stir the ingredients together until well combined and smooth. If the sauce seems too thick, gradually add a bit more water until you reach your desired consistency.
3. **Adjust Flavors:**
    - Taste the sauce and adjust the flavors as needed. Add more soy sauce for saltiness, lime juice for tanginess, brown sugar or honey for sweetness, or sriracha for spiciness.
4. **Optional Creaminess:**
    - For a creamier sauce, stir in a tablespoon of coconut milk. This adds richness and balances the flavors.
5. **Serve or Store:**
    - Use the peanut sauce immediately as a dip for satay skewers, spring rolls, or drizzled over noodles and salads.
    - If not using immediately, store the sauce in an airtight container in the refrigerator for up to one week.

Notes:

- **Consistency:** Adjust the amount of water to achieve your preferred thickness. Remember that the sauce will thicken slightly when refrigerated.
- **Spice Level:** Customize the spiciness by adjusting the amount of sriracha sauce or adding chopped fresh chili peppers.
- **Allergies:** If you have peanut allergies, you can substitute peanut butter with almond butter or sunflower seed butter for a different flavor profile.

Enjoy your homemade Thai Peanut Sauce with your favorite dishes! It adds a delightful burst of flavor and richness to any meal.

Thai Steamed Fish with Lime and Garlic

Ingredients:

- 2 fish fillets (such as tilapia, seabass, or snapper), about 6-8 oz each
- 3 cloves garlic, thinly sliced
- 1-2 Thai bird's eye chilies, thinly sliced (adjust to spice preference)
- 1/4 cup fresh lime juice
- 2 tablespoons fish sauce
- 1 tablespoon soy sauce
- 1 tablespoon brown sugar or palm sugar
- 1/4 cup cilantro leaves, chopped (for garnish)
- Thinly sliced spring onions (scallions), for garnish
- Fresh cilantro sprigs, for garnish
- Thinly sliced fresh chili (optional, for garnish)

Instructions:

1. **Prepare the Steamer:**
    - Set up a steamer large enough to fit the fish fillets. Make sure the water is boiling or steaming before placing the fish in the steamer.
2. **Prepare the Fish:**
    - Place the fish fillets on a heatproof dish or plate that fits inside the steamer. Score the fish a few times on each side with a sharp knife. This helps the flavors penetrate the fish.
3. **Make the Sauce:**
    - In a small bowl, combine the fresh lime juice, fish sauce, soy sauce, and brown sugar (or palm sugar). Stir well until the sugar is dissolved.
4. **Steam the Fish:**
    - Spread half of the sliced garlic and chili over the fish fillets. Reserve the other half for garnish.
    - Pour half of the lime and sauce mixture evenly over the fish fillets.
5. **Steam the fish:** Cover the steamer and steam the fish for about 8-10 minutes, or until the fish is cooked through and flakes easily with a fork.

Thai Beef Noodle Soup (Kuay Teow Neua)

Ingredients:

- 250g rice noodles (flat or thin)
- 300g beef (sirloin or flank), thinly sliced
- 4 cups beef broth (homemade or store-bought)
- 2 cups water
- 3 cloves garlic, minced
- 1-inch piece of ginger, sliced
- 2-3 shallots, thinly sliced
- 1-2 tablespoons vegetable oil
- 1 tablespoon soy sauce
- 1 tablespoon fish sauce
- 1 tablespoon oyster sauce
- 1 teaspoon sugar
- 1 star anise (optional)
- 1 cinnamon stick (optional)
- 1 teaspoon ground coriander (optional)
- Salt and pepper, to taste
- Fresh cilantro leaves, chopped, for garnish
- Fresh Thai basil leaves, for garnish
- Bean sprouts, for garnish
- Lime wedges, for serving
- Chili flakes or sliced fresh chili, for serving (optional)

Instructions:

1. **Prepare the Beef:**
   - Marinate the beef slices with soy sauce, fish sauce, and a pinch of pepper. Set aside while you prepare the other ingredients.
2. **Prepare the Broth:**
   - In a large pot, heat the vegetable oil over medium heat. Add the minced garlic, ginger slices, and shallots. Stir-fry until fragrant, about 1-2 minutes.
3. **Simmer the Broth:**
   - Pour in the beef broth and water. Add the star anise, cinnamon stick, and ground coriander (if using). Bring to a boil, then reduce the heat and let it simmer for about 15-20 minutes to develop flavors. Remove the star anise and cinnamon stick before serving.
4. **Cook the Noodles:**
   - While the broth simmers, cook the rice noodles according to package instructions until al dente. Drain and rinse under cold water to prevent sticking. Set aside.
5. **Cook the Beef:**

- In a separate pan, heat a bit of oil over medium-high heat. Add the marinated beef slices and stir-fry quickly until just cooked, about 2-3 minutes. Remove from heat and set aside.

6. **Season the Broth:**
    - Season the broth with oyster sauce, sugar, and salt to taste. Adjust the seasoning with more soy sauce or fish sauce if needed.

7. **Assemble the Soup:**
    - Divide the cooked noodles among serving bowls. Top with the cooked beef slices.

8. **Serve:**
    - Ladle the hot broth over the noodles and beef. Garnish with fresh cilantro leaves, Thai basil leaves, bean sprouts, and a squeeze of lime juice.
    - Serve immediately, with chili flakes or sliced fresh chili on the side for those who enjoy extra heat.

Enjoy your comforting and aromatic Thai Beef Noodle Soup! It's perfect for a satisfying meal any time of the year.

Thai Omelette (Kai Jeow)

Ingredients:

- 2-3 large eggs
- 1-2 tablespoons fish sauce
- 1 tablespoon soy sauce
- 1 tablespoon oyster sauce (optional)
- 1 teaspoon sugar
- Vegetable oil, for frying
- Fresh cilantro leaves, chopped (for garnish)
- Thai chili sauce or Sriracha, for serving (optional)

Instructions:

1. **Prepare the Egg Mixture:**
    - In a bowl, crack the eggs and beat them lightly with a fork or whisk. Add fish sauce, soy sauce, oyster sauce (if using), and sugar. Mix well until the ingredients are combined.
2. **Heat the Oil:**
    - Heat vegetable oil in a non-stick skillet or frying pan over medium-high heat. Make sure the oil is hot enough to sizzle when you add the egg mixture.
3. **Fry the Omelette:**
    - Pour the egg mixture into the heated skillet. Tilt the pan to spread the egg evenly into a round shape. Let it cook undisturbed for about 1-2 minutes, or until the edges start to set and the bottom is golden brown.
4. **Flip the Omelette (optional):**
    - If desired, carefully flip the omelette using a spatula to cook the other side for another 1-2 minutes. Alternatively, you can leave it as is for a fluffy texture without flipping.
5. **Serve:**
    - Transfer the omelette to a serving plate. Garnish with chopped cilantro leaves.
6. **Enjoy:**
    - Serve hot with jasmine rice and Thai chili sauce or Sriracha on the side for extra flavor.

Tips:

- **Variations:** You can add other ingredients to the egg mixture such as chopped onions, tomatoes, or even minced meat for different flavors and textures.
- **Cooking Technique:** The key to a perfect Thai omelette is cooking it quickly over medium-high heat to achieve a crispy outer layer while keeping the inside fluffy.
- **Serving:** Thai omelette is often served as part of a larger meal with rice and other dishes, but it can also be enjoyed on its own as a snack or light meal.

Enjoy your homemade Thai omelette (Kai Jeow)!

Thai Coconut Pudding (Tub Tim Grob)

Ingredients:

- 1 cup water chestnuts, peeled and diced into small cubes
- Red food coloring (optional)
- 1 tablespoon tapioca flour or cornstarch
- 1 cup coconut milk
- 1/2 cup water
- 1/4 cup sugar
- Crushed ice, for serving

Optional Toppings:

- Jackfruit slices
- Young coconut meat
- Sweetened condensed milk

Instructions:

1. **Prepare the Red Rubies (Tub Tim Grob):**
   - In a bowl, mix the diced water chestnuts with a few drops of red food coloring (if using) until they are evenly coated. This step is optional but adds color to the dessert.
   - Add tapioca flour or cornstarch to the water chestnuts and mix well to coat them evenly.
2. **Cook the Red Rubies:**
   - Bring a pot of water to boil. Add the coated water chestnuts and cook until they float to the surface (about 2-3 minutes). Once they float, remove them from the boiling water and rinse them under cold water to stop the cooking process. Set aside.
3. **Prepare the Coconut Syrup:**
   - In another pot, combine the coconut milk, water, and sugar. Bring to a gentle boil over medium heat, stirring occasionally until the sugar dissolves. Remove from heat and let it cool down.
4. **Assemble the Dessert:**
   - To serve, divide the cooked red rubies (Tub Tim Grob) into serving bowls or glasses.
   - Pour the chilled coconut syrup over the red rubies.
5. **Add Toppings (Optional):**
   - Top the dessert with crushed ice for a refreshing texture.
   - Optionally, garnish with jackfruit slices, young coconut meat, or a drizzle of sweetened condensed milk.
6. **Serve:**

- Serve the Thai Coconut Pudding (Tub Tim Grob) cold as a refreshing dessert.

Notes:

- **Preparation Tips:** It's important to rinse the cooked red rubies (water chestnuts) under cold water to maintain their texture and prevent them from sticking together.
- **Variations:** Some recipes include adding coconut jelly or pandan-flavored tapioca pearls to enhance the flavor and texture of the dessert.
- **Storage:** Store any leftovers in the refrigerator and consume within a day or two for the best taste and texture.

Enjoy making and serving this Thai Coconut Pudding (Tub Tim Grob) for a delightful and cooling dessert on a hot day!

Thai Spicy Pork Salad (Nam Tok Moo)

Ingredients:

- 300g pork loin or pork shoulder, thinly sliced or cut into bite-sized pieces
- 1/4 cup roasted rice powder (Khao Khua) *(See Note)*
- 2-3 shallots, thinly sliced
- 2-3 spring onions (scallions), thinly sliced
- 1-2 tablespoons chopped fresh cilantro
- 1-2 tablespoons chopped fresh mint leaves
- 2-3 tablespoons fish sauce
- 2-3 tablespoons lime juice
- 1-2 teaspoons palm sugar or brown sugar
- 1-2 tablespoons roasted chili powder (adjust to spice preference)
- Fresh lettuce leaves, cucumber slices, and Thai basil for serving

Instructions:

1. **Prepare the Pork:**
   - Heat a grill pan or skillet over medium-high heat. Cook the pork slices until they are cooked through and slightly charred, about 3-4 minutes per side. Alternatively, you can grill the pork outdoors if preferred. Once cooked, let it rest for a few minutes before slicing thinly.
2. **Make the Dressing:**
   - In a mixing bowl, combine fish sauce, lime juice, palm sugar (or brown sugar), and roasted chili powder. Adjust the seasoning to your taste by balancing the salty, sour, and sweet flavors.
3. **Assemble the Salad:**
   - In a large mixing bowl, combine the sliced grilled pork, shallots, spring onions, cilantro, and mint leaves.
   - Pour the prepared dressing over the pork mixture and toss gently to coat everything evenly.
4. **Add Roasted Rice Powder:**
   - Sprinkle roasted rice powder (Khao Khua) over the salad and mix well. The rice powder adds a nutty flavor and helps absorb the dressing.
5. **Serve:**
   - Arrange fresh lettuce leaves and cucumber slices on a serving platter. Transfer the Nam Tok Moo salad onto the platter.
   - Garnish with additional fresh herbs like Thai basil leaves.
   - Serve immediately as a salad or with sticky rice on the side.

Notes:

- **Roasted Rice Powder (Khao Khua):** To make roasted rice powder, dry roast uncooked sticky rice in a pan until golden brown and fragrant. Grind the roasted rice in a mortar and pestle or a spice grinder until it becomes a coarse powder.
- **Variations:** Some recipes may include toasted ground rice powder in the dressing for added texture, or toasted crushed peanuts for extra crunch.
- **Spice Level:** Adjust the amount of roasted chili powder according to your preference for spiciness.

Nam Tok Moo is a flavorful and satisfying Thai dish that balances spicy, sour, and savory flavors with tender grilled pork. Enjoy it as a refreshing salad or as a main dish with sticky rice for a complete meal.

Thai Stir-Fried Tofu with Basil

Ingredients:

- 1 block (about 14 oz) firm tofu, drained and cut into cubes
- 2 tablespoons vegetable oil
- 4-5 cloves garlic, minced
- 2-3 Thai bird's eye chilies, thinly sliced (adjust to spice preference)
- 1 bell pepper, sliced (optional for added color and crunch)
- 1 onion, sliced
- 1 cup fresh basil leaves, preferably Thai basil
- 1 tablespoon soy sauce
- 1 tablespoon oyster sauce (optional for added umami)
- 1 tablespoon fish sauce
- 1 teaspoon sugar
- Freshly ground black pepper, to taste
- Cooked jasmine rice, for serving

Instructions:

1. **Prepare the Tofu:**
   - Drain the tofu and cut it into cubes. Pat dry with paper towels to remove excess moisture.
2. **Stir-Fry the Tofu:**
   - Heat vegetable oil in a large skillet or wok over medium-high heat. Add the tofu cubes and stir-fry until they are golden brown and slightly crispy on all sides. Remove tofu from the skillet and set aside.
3. **Stir-Fry the Aromatics:**
   - In the same skillet, add a bit more oil if needed. Add minced garlic and sliced Thai bird's eye chilies. Stir-fry for about 1 minute until fragrant.
4. **Add Vegetables (optional):**
   - Add sliced bell pepper and onion to the skillet. Stir-fry for another 2-3 minutes until the vegetables are tender-crisp.
5. **Combine Sauce:**
   - In a small bowl, mix together soy sauce, oyster sauce (if using), fish sauce, sugar, and black pepper.
6. **Combine Tofu and Sauce:**
   - Return the cooked tofu to the skillet. Pour the prepared sauce over the tofu and vegetables. Stir-fry for another minute or until everything is well coated and heated through.
7. **Add Basil Leaves:**
   - Add fresh basil leaves to the skillet. Toss everything together for about 30 seconds to allow the basil leaves to wilt slightly and release their aroma.
8. **Serve:**

- Remove from heat and serve hot over cooked jasmine rice.

Notes:

- **Variations:** Feel free to customize this dish by adding other vegetables such as broccoli, carrots, or snap peas.
- **Spice Level:** Adjust the amount of Thai bird's eye chilies according to your preference for spiciness.
- **Vegetarian/Vegan Option:** Omit the oyster sauce or replace it with vegetarian oyster sauce to make this dish vegetarian or vegan.

Enjoy your flavorful and aromatic Thai Stir-Fried Tofu with Basil (Pad Krapow Tofu)! It's a quick and satisfying dish that pairs wonderfully with jasmine rice.

Thai Chicken Curry Noodles (Khao Soi Gai)

Ingredients:

For the Khao Soi Paste:

- 4-6 dried red chilies, soaked in hot water to soften
- 4 cloves garlic
- 1 shallot, chopped
- 1-inch piece of ginger, peeled and chopped
- 1 tablespoon ground coriander
- 1 tablespoon ground turmeric
- 1 teaspoon shrimp paste (optional, but recommended for depth of flavor)
- 1 stalk lemongrass, white part only, chopped
- 2 tablespoons vegetable oil

For the Curry:

- 2 tablespoons vegetable oil
- 1 pound boneless, skinless chicken thighs or breasts, thinly sliced
- 2 cans (14 oz each) coconut milk
- 2 cups chicken broth
- 2 tablespoons soy sauce
- 1 tablespoon palm sugar or brown sugar
- Salt, to taste

For Serving:

- 1 pound fresh egg noodles, cooked according to package instructions
- Fresh cilantro, chopped
- Red onion, thinly sliced
- Lime wedges
- Crispy fried egg noodles (optional, for garnish)

Instructions:

1. **Prepare the Khao Soi Paste:**
    - In a blender or food processor, combine soaked dried red chilies (remove seeds for less heat if desired), garlic, shallot, ginger, ground coriander, ground turmeric, shrimp paste (if using), and chopped lemongrass. Blend until you get a smooth paste consistency.
2. **Cook the Curry:**
    - Heat vegetable oil in a large pot over medium heat. Add the Khao Soi paste and cook for 2-3 minutes, stirring constantly until fragrant.
    - Add chicken slices to the pot and cook until the chicken is browned on all sides.

3. **Add Coconut Milk and Broth:**
   - Pour in coconut milk and chicken broth. Stir well to combine. Bring the mixture to a boil, then reduce heat and let it simmer uncovered for about 20-25 minutes until the chicken is cooked through and tender.
4. **Season the Curry:**
   - Stir in soy sauce and palm sugar (or brown sugar). Season with salt to taste. Adjust seasoning if needed.
5. **Prepare the Noodles:**
   - While the curry is simmering, cook fresh egg noodles according to package instructions. Drain and set aside.
6. **Serve Khao Soi:**
   - To serve, divide the cooked egg noodles among serving bowls.
   - Ladle the hot Khao Soi curry over the noodles.
   - Garnish with chopped fresh cilantro, thinly sliced red onion, and a squeeze of lime juice.
   - Optionally, top with crispy fried egg noodles for added texture.
7. **Enjoy:**
   - Serve Khao Soi Gai immediately while hot, and enjoy the rich and comforting flavors of this Northern Thai curry noodle dish.

Notes:

- **Variations:** Khao Soi can also be made with beef or tofu instead of chicken. Adjust cooking times accordingly based on the protein used.
- **Spice Level:** Adjust the amount of dried red chilies in the Khao Soi paste to suit your preference for spiciness.
- **Storage:** Leftover Khao Soi can be stored in an airtight container in the refrigerator for up to 3 days. Reheat gently on the stove before serving.

Enjoy making and savoring this authentic Thai Chicken Curry Noodles (Khao Soi Gai) at home! It's a wonderful dish that combines creamy coconut curry with tender chicken and noodles, perfect for any occasion.

Thai Green Bean Salad

Ingredients:

For the Salad:

- 300g green beans, trimmed and cut into 2-inch pieces
- 1 red bell pepper, thinly sliced
- 1/2 cup cherry tomatoes, halved
- 1/4 cup thinly sliced red onion
- 1/4 cup roasted peanuts, roughly chopped
- Fresh cilantro leaves for garnish
- Fresh Thai basil leaves for garnish (optional)

For the Dressing:

- 2 tablespoons fish sauce
- 2 tablespoons lime juice
- 1 tablespoon palm sugar or brown sugar
- 1-2 Thai bird's eye chilies, finely chopped (adjust to spice preference)
- 2 cloves garlic, minced

Instructions:

1. **Blanch the Green Beans:**
   - Bring a pot of water to a boil. Add the green beans and blanch for about 2-3 minutes, or until they are crisp-tender. Drain and rinse under cold water to stop the cooking process. Set aside.
2. **Prepare the Dressing:**
   - In a small bowl, whisk together fish sauce, lime juice, palm sugar, chopped Thai bird's eye chilies, and minced garlic until the sugar is dissolved.
3. **Assemble the Salad:**
   - In a large mixing bowl, combine blanched green beans, sliced red bell pepper, halved cherry tomatoes, and sliced red onion.
4. **Add the Dressing:**
   - Pour the prepared dressing over the salad ingredients. Toss gently to coat everything evenly with the dressing.
5. **Garnish:**
   - Sprinkle chopped roasted peanuts over the salad.
   - Garnish with fresh cilantro leaves and Thai basil leaves (if using) for added freshness and flavor.
6. **Serve:**
   - Transfer the Thai Green Bean Salad to a serving dish or individual plates.
   - Serve immediately as a refreshing side dish or as a light meal on its own.

Notes:

- **Variations:** You can add grilled shrimp, chicken, or tofu to make this salad a complete meal.
- **Make-Ahead:** You can blanch the green beans and prepare the dressing ahead of time. Assemble the salad just before serving to maintain its freshness.
- **Spice Level:** Adjust the amount of Thai bird's eye chilies according to your preference for spiciness.

This Thai Green Bean Salad (Yum Tua Poo) is bursting with flavors of Thailand—tangy lime, spicy chilies, and fresh herbs—making it a perfect dish for summer or any time you crave a refreshing and vibrant salad.

Thai Pineapple Fried Rice

Ingredients:

- 2 cups cooked jasmine rice, preferably cooled or day-old
- 1 cup fresh pineapple, diced into small pieces
- 1 red bell pepper, diced
- 1 small onion, diced
- 2-3 cloves garlic, minced
- 1-2 Thai bird's eye chilies, finely chopped (optional, adjust to spice preference)
- 1/2 cup frozen peas and carrots mix (thawed)
- 2 eggs, beaten
- 1/2 cup cooked chicken, shrimp, or tofu (optional)
- 2 tablespoons vegetable oil
- 2 tablespoons soy sauce
- 1 tablespoon fish sauce
- 1 tablespoon oyster sauce (optional)
- 1 tablespoon curry powder (yellow or Madras)
- 1/2 teaspoon sugar
- Fresh cilantro leaves for garnish
- Lime wedges for serving

Instructions:

1. **Prepare the Ingredients:**
   - If you haven't already, cook the jasmine rice and allow it to cool down. Day-old rice works best for fried rice as it is drier and less sticky.
2. **Stir-Fry the Aromatics:**
   - Heat vegetable oil in a large skillet or wok over medium-high heat. Add minced garlic and chopped Thai bird's eye chilies (if using). Stir-fry for about 30 seconds until fragrant.
3. **Cook the Eggs:**
   - Push the garlic and chilies to one side of the skillet. Pour beaten eggs into the empty side and scramble them until they are cooked through.
4. **Add Protein and Vegetables:**
   - If using, add cooked chicken, shrimp, or tofu to the skillet. Stir-fry briefly until heated through.
5. **Stir-Fry Rice and Vegetables:**
   - Add diced red bell pepper, onion, and thawed peas and carrots mix to the skillet. Stir-fry for 2-3 minutes until the vegetables are tender-crisp.
6. **Add Pineapple and Seasonings:**
   - Add diced pineapple pieces to the skillet. Stir in soy sauce, fish sauce, oyster sauce (if using), curry powder, and sugar. Mix well to combine all ingredients evenly.

7. **Add Rice:**
   - Add the cooked jasmine rice to the skillet. Using a spatula or wooden spoon, gently stir-fry everything together until the rice is heated through and well-coated with the seasonings. Break up any clumps of rice as you stir.
8. **Finish and Serve:**
   - Taste and adjust seasoning if needed, adding more soy sauce or fish sauce according to your preference.
   - Remove from heat and garnish with fresh cilantro leaves.
   - Serve Thai Pineapple Fried Rice hot, with lime wedges on the side for squeezing over the rice before eating.

Notes:

- **Variations:** You can add other ingredients like cashew nuts, raisins, or different vegetables such as baby corn or snow peas.
- **Make-Ahead:** Prepare all the ingredients ahead of time and cook them quickly in the skillet just before serving for best results.
- **Vegetarian/Vegan Option:** Omit the eggs and use tofu or extra vegetables for a vegetarian or vegan version.

Enjoy this delicious Thai Pineapple Fried Rice as a flavorful and satisfying meal that brings a taste of Thailand to your table!

www.ingramcontent.com/pod-product-compliance
Lightning Source LLC
LaVergne TN
LVHW081608060526
838201LV00054B/2135